LEARNING THROUGH FIELD

A Developmental Approach

Susan F. Cochrane
College of St. Catherine

Marla Martin Hanley
College of St. Catherine

Allyn and Bacon
Boston London Toronto Sydney Tokyo Singapore

Copyright © 1999 by Allyn & Bacon
A Viacom Company
160 Gould Street
Needham Heights, Massachusetts 02194-2130

Internet: www.abacon.com

Library of Congress Cataloging-in-Publication Data

Cochrane, Susan F.
    Learning through field : a developmental approach / Susan F.
Cochrane, Marla Martin Hanley.
        p.   cm.
    Includes index.
    ISBN 0-205-26809-9
    1. Social work education--United States. 2. Social service--Field
work--Study and teaching--United States.   I. Hanley, Marla Martin.
II. Title.
HV11.C71137   1998
361.3'2'071--dc21   98-18643
                                                                  CIP

Printed in the United States of America

10 9 8 7 6 5 4 3 2   03 02 01 00 99

Our deepest gratitude to

Serene Thornton
for her partnership in creating the original developmental model

Barbara Shank
for her passionate commitment to field education

Our students
and field instructors
for teaching us through their field experiences

Our faculty colleagues
for their wisdom & encouragement-
especially Barb Berger, Mary Carlsen, Randy Herman, & Sandy Parnell
for their contributions to this book

Meghan Kennedy & Jeanette Zachowski
for valuable research assistance and manuscript preparation

and our families
for their love and support

Contents

Acknowledgments

Introduction:
The Developmental Stages in Field Education   xi
How to Use This Book   xiii
Developmental Stages in Field Chart   xvi

Stage 1 - Beginning

Chapter 1: Preparing to Learn   **2**
Stage 1 Chart   2
Vignettes   3
Developmental Features   4
Integration and Application   5
What is Field?   6
What to Expect From Others   8
What to Expect From Yourself   10
Journal Assignments   15
Table 1.1 Check Out Your Fit With Social Work   17
Seminar Activities   18
References   19
Additional Readings   19

Chapter 2: Planning Your Orientation   **20**
Stage 1 Chart   20
Vignette   21
Developmental Features   22
The Value of Planned Orientation   23
Micro Level of Orientation   24
Table 2.1 Orientation Plan   26
Mezzo Level of Orientation   28
Macro Level of Orientation   29
Journal Assignments   32
Seminar Activities   33
Form 2.1 Beginning Agreement   35
Form 2.2 Agency Presentation Outline   37
Reference   39
Additional Readings   39

Chapter 3: Focusing Your Learning   **40**
Stage 1 Chart   40
Vignettes   41
Developmental Features   42
Assess Program Requirements   43
Assess Agency Possibilities   43

Assess Personal Needs 44
Table 3.1 Learning Contract 45
Planning a Learning Contract 47
Journal Assignments 51
Seminar Activities 51
Form 3.1 Learning Contract 53
Additional Readings 55

Chapter 4: Beginning the Work   **5 6**
Stage 1 Chart 56
Vignette 57
Developmental Features 58
Tuning In 58
Explaining Your Role 61
Prepare to Listen for Unspoken Messages 62
Review Your Work 63
Journal Assignments 65
Seminar Activities 66
Form 4.1 Work Presentation 67
Reference 69
Additional Readings 69

Stage 2 - Reality Confrontation

Chapter 5: Building Skills in Supervision and Feedback 7 0
Stage 2 Chart 70
Vignette 71
Developmental Features 72
Understanding Supervision 72
Feedback: A Central Skill 78
Table 5.1 SPIN: Guidelines for Feedback 79
Journal Assignments 81
Seminar Activities 81
Additional Readings 82

Chapter 6: Confronting Difficult Issues   **8 4**
Stage 2 Chart 84
Vignettes 85
Developmental Features 86
Why Confront Difficult Issues? 87
Table 6.1 Examples of Difficult Issues 88
The Importance of Using Consultation 89
Skills for Confronting Difficult Issues 91
    Sexual Harassment 95
    Changing Field Instructors 96
    Changing Agencies 97
    Leaving the Social Work Program 98
Journal Assignments 100
Form 6.1 Evaluating Your Group Participation 101
Seminar Activities 102
Form 6.2 Peer Consultation Request 105

References   107
Additional Readings   107

Stage 3 - Relative Mastery

Chapter 7: Shaping a Professional Self   **108**
Stage 3 Chart   108
Vignettes   109
Developmental Features   110
Moving Toward a More Aware Practice   111
Table 7.1 Developing a Personal Style   114
Moving Toward a More Active Practice   115
Table 7.2 Markers of Active Practice   117
Moving Toward a More Analytical Practice   118
Table 7.3 Seven Step Model of Ethical Decision Making   119
Journal Assignments   124
Seminar Activities   124
Form 7.1 Professional Behavior Checklist   127
References   129
Additional Readings   129

Chapter 8: Taking Risks   **132**
Stage 3 Chart   132
Vignette   133
Developmental Features   133
Workplace Differences   134
Table 8.1 Cultural Competence Continuum   136
Workplace Dynamics   137
Workplace Skills   139
Journal Assignments   143
Seminar Activities   143
Reference   145
Additional Readings   145

Stage 4 - Closure

Chapter 9: Ending and Looking Ahead   **146**
Stage 4 Chart   146
Vignette   147
Developmental Features   148
Handling Endings   149
Process of Termination   150
Moving On: Life beyond Field   151
Table 9.1 Tasks for Termination   152
Journal Assignments   157
Seminar Activities   158
Additional Readings   159
Form 9.1 Field Evaluation   161

Appendices   167

Appendix   A: Steps to Finding a Field Placement   168
Appendix   B: Interviewing with an Agency   169
Appendix   C: Application for Social Work Field Position 172
Appendix   D: Field Practicum in Place of Employment   174
Appendix   E: Decision Map   178
Appendix   F: Codes of Ethics   180

Index   *184*

Journal Assignments

1.1	Preparing an Inventory of Personal Strengths	15
1.2	Identifying Support Systems	15
1.3	Starting to Think about Personal Issues	15
1.4	Identifying Learning Style	16
2.1	Anticipating the First Day	32
2.2	Revisiting Learning Style	32
2.3	Thinking about Supervision	32
2.4	Reflecting on Seminar Participation	32
3.1	Addressing Strengths and Vulnerabilities	51
3.2	Thinking about a Learning Contract	51
4.1	Reflecting on Highs and Lows	65
4.2	Explaining Your Role	65
4.3	Exploring Value Differences	65
5.1	Thinking about Support	81
5.2	Thinking about Authority and Power	81
5.3	Reflecting on Seminar Participation	81
6.1	Beginning a Stress Journal	100
6.2	Reflecting on Highs and Lows	100
6.3	Evaluating Your Group Participation	100
7.1	Exploring Personal History	124
7.2	Exploring Personal Style	124
7.3	Exploring Personal Meaning	124
7.4	Reviewing Professional Behavior	124
8.1	Measuring Personal Cultural Competence	143
8.2	Improving Workplace Relationships	143
8.3	Analyzing Agency Policy	143
9.1	Reflecting on Past Endings	157
9.2	Updating Your Self-Assessment	157
9.3	Reviewing and Planning	157
9.4	Updating Support System	157
9.5	Networking	158

Seminar Activities

1.1	Using Ice Breakers	18
1.2	Creating a Safe Seminar Atmosphere	18
1.3	Discussing Learning Styles	19
2.1	Discussing Your First Day	33
2.2	Checking In	33
2.3	Making an Agency Presentation	33
3.1	Drafting a Learning Goal	52
3.2	Discussing a Sample Contract	52
3.3	Integrating Resources on Diversity	52
4.1	Presenting Your Work	66
4.2	Identifying Social Work Roles	66
4.3	Integrating Coursework and Field	66
5.1	Role-Playing Feedback	81
5.2	Discussing Supervision	81
5.3	Discussing Midpoint Evaluation	82
6.1	Whining Together	102
6.2	Role Playing Difficult Situations	102
6.3	Using Peer Consultation	102
6.4	Evaluating Group	102
7.1	Discussing Personal Styles	124
7.2	Using the Seven Step Ethical Model	125
7.3	Using Consultation	125
7.4	Applying Research Articles	125
7.5	Discussing Practice Evaluation	125
7.6	Discussing the Human Condition	125
8.1	Measuring Agency Cultural Competence	143
8.2	Consulting about Workplace Relationships	144
8.3	Analyzing Agency Challenges	144
8.4	Integrating Coursework and Field	144
8.5	Impacting Agencies	144
8.6	Using the Internet	144
9.1	Ending Seminar Group	158
9.2	Role Playing Agency Endings	158
9.3	Role Playing Job Interviews	158
9.4	Informational Interviewing	158
9.5	Writing a Resume	159

Introduction

Welcome to social work and to "field." We believe field is the heart of social work education - the essential place where your knowledge, skills, experiences, feelings, and values all come together - an exciting, challenging, sometimes frightening place. Our goal for this book is to help students discover, understand, and benefit from the developmental process of field education, a process that has much in common with other types of learning.

Consider the time and patience required to learn a musical instrument or a sport. Progress can be slow and barriers can seem daunting, but each small step toward mastery brings increased confidence and motivation. Social workers experience a similar developmental process in their own professional growth, beginning with their field education. Research has helped us to understand many aspects of the process of field education. Cochrane and Thornton (1990, 1992) conducted an empirical study with junior, senior, and first year graduate students in which students completed weekly questionnaires during their year-long field placements. The data describe a developmental process with fairly predictable stages, each with highs and lows, stressors and possible coping mechanisms.

Naturally, since each learner is unique, each social work student may not experience phases of field development in exactly the same way. Students need to develop knowledge of how they, as individuals, tend to respond to others, to new situations, to learning. However, as we have shared and discussed this model with many students through the years, it has assisted them to anticipate what stages they might experience and what challenges they might expect. Students can be reassured that they are not alone in their feelings as their practicum progresses, and they can sometimes prepare and adjust in more thoughtful ways as they anticipate what may lie ahead.

The Developmental Stages In Field Education

The stages of development in field that students have described to us are similar to many other processes. Usually, students begin in a honeymoon phase, in which the agency and field instructor seem exciting and wonderful. Then follows a crash when nothing seems to go right and things are not as easy as they originally seemed. This "let down" can be so disappointing that many students want to change to a new placement rather than face the realities of the present one. However, when students work through the disappointments, explore the possibilities, and develop a plan of action, they usually gain renewed commitment to learn and confront challenges. This difficult work brings students to a phase in which they feel more competent and can finish the practicum feeling proud and confident. The chart on pages vi-vii describes the four stages that comprise the process of field education. You may want to refer to this chart as your practicum progresses, to remind yourself of what you have experienced, as well as to prepare yourself for what may be coming.

We find that these stages in field tend to be similar for juniors, seniors, and beginning graduate students, regardless of age or experience. While the progression of stages tends to be fairly predictable, each individual student may differ in the length of the stage and its particular anxieties and stresses. Juniors tend to stay longer in the honeymoon phase; their comfort level is often low and they need more time to move into field assignments or responsibilities that may test their early perceptions. Seniors may feel more anxious in the termination phase because of the additional pressures of looking for employment, considering graduate school, or other transitions that accompany graduation. People who have been in the work world before returning to school experience the stress of transition to a student status, which compounds the initial stages of adjustment to the field placement. Students with experience, however, may move more quickly through the first stage and may have more resources for handling challenges. With all students, however, comfort level is generally lower when facing new tasks, but confidence increases when a task has been mastered.

Much of this developmental model deals with various types of stress students may encounter during the practicum. Stress is a natural part of life; it is a natural part of a field placement, too. Frequently, students report that the first day, the first staff meeting, and the first client are all very anxiety provoking. For each of us, an important part of learning to be a social worker is discovering what we find particularly stressing, what is unique in our response to stress, and what positive steps we can then take to handle that stress. Please be open to learning and using healthy coping strategies during your practicum experience so that you can deal with the challenges inherent in professional practice.

How To Use This Book

Each social work or human services program has a unique plan for incorporating field education into the curriculum. This book is designed to be used by programs whose students are in an agency placement and, at the same time, have a seminar for discussing field issues. It also is used as a supplemental text in programs that incorporate field education into a practice class. This book is not designed to be a practice, policy, research, or human behavior text; rather, it is designed to encourage you to integrate content from those classes into your field experience.

This book may be adapted for many types of field programs because the process students experience is the same. The chapter material, discussion topics, and journal assignments focus on this process rather than on the "mechanics" of field education, which vary greatly between programs. For example, information about interviewing and choosing a placement is available in the appendix for those students who may need it, but Chapter One focuses on clarifying roles and expectations, which are tasks common to every beginning student.

A word about the organization of the chapters. A section of the developmental stages in field is inserted before every chapter for easy reference. Items that will be discussed in the chapter have been highlighted with bullets. Each chapter then begins with questions or comments we have heard from students at certain points in their practicum. Vignettes or a short case study highlight the themes of the chapter. Concepts and skills are presented, as well as suggestions for journaling and in-class group activities. Ideas for further reading are included at the end of each chapter. Depending on the length of your practicum, some chapters may take weeks to discuss; others might only take a short time. You may want to revisit chapters or glance ahead to find a specific discussion helpful to you at a particular time.

Each chapter includes field journal exercises to help you reflect on your learning through field. These exercises may also help you sort through challenging experiences, increase your self-awareness, and sound out new ideas. Journal writing may also help you prepare for discussions with your faculty liaison, other students, or your field instructor. We encourage you to find a comfortable space and time in which to write a journal. Date each entry and include the topic of the assignment to make your record easier to refer back to in the future. Whether you use a computer or pen and notebook, leave the backs of pages blank for your comments as you revisit earlier entries. We encourage you, also, to share specific portions of your field journal with your faculty liaison so that you have feedback on your program.

Learning through Field, as we have shown, is built on the idea that field is a developmental process. Each chapter, in its discussion and activities, addresses the challenges of each stage and suggests ways to handle those challenges. By anticipating the process, most students become less anxious about how they may respond, can plan to secure the support they will need, and can have more realistic expectations of the agency and of themselves. We hope this book will help you to make the most of your field experience as you become more competent and confident social workers.

REFERENCES:

Cochrane, S., & Thornton, S. (1990). The process of adjustment in field placement: Implications for baccalaureate field educators. In K.J. Kazmerski (Ed.), *Proceedings of the Eighth Annual BPD Conference*, 61-70.

Cochrane, S., & Thornton, S. (1992, March). *Differential adjustment to practicum settings for graduate and undergraduate students*. Paper presented at the 38th Annual Program Meeting, Council on Social Work Education, Kansas City, MO.

Developmental Stages in Field

Stage 1:   Beginning

<u>Students Report:</u>
    Feeling like a stranger, then a guest
    Feeling vulnerable and self-conscious
    Being enthusiastic about assignments, yet fearful
    Feeling anxious about meeting other staff
    Feeling overwhelmed

<u>Students Need:</u>
    A safe place to share concerns with seminar members and faculty liaison
    Permission to be learners; to understand learning styles
    To build self-awareness of strengths and limitations
    To identify support systems
    To discuss feelings and questions with field instructor
    To be introduced at the agency, to have a place to sit, to leave coat, papers
    Clarification of roles, expectations, and policies
    A written orientation plan
    A plan to focus goals and meet general requirements
    To individualize placement
    To understand how to use supervision in planning and reviewing work
    Skills to start work assignments

Stage 2:   Reality Confrontation

<u>Students Report:</u>
    Stress: often get the flu or a cold, become a bit depressed
    Becoming disillusioned with agency, field instructor, social work classes
    Wondering if social work is a good fit for them
    Wondering if social workers can do any good
    Sometimes wanting to give up or change placements

<u>Students Need:</u>
    To talk with peers, field instructor, and faculty liaison about doubts and
        fears
    To reflect on how they handle stressful situations; to use stress
        management skills
    To examine their expectations of themselves
    Permission to make mistakes and take risks
    To identify discomforts with agency, field instructors, social work
        profession
    Assistance with major problems, crises, and decisions
    To explore feelings about support, authority, independence
    To build a solid supervisory relationship with field instructor
    Effective supervisory conferences
    Skills in feedback

Stage 3:   Relative Mastery

<u>Students Report:</u>
Feeling more confident and competent
Learning to leave worries at the agency
Continued anxiety about new assignments, working with clients
Reaching a compromise between reality and expectations
Willingness to discuss value dilemmas

<u>Students Need:</u>
To take more initiative in own learning, become more self-directed
To explore new challenges
To continue building relationship with field instructor
To evaluate more concrete feedback
To evaluate own practice
To build on strengths and interests
To identify what learning they still need
To find ways to contribute to the agency

Stage 4:   Closure

<u>Students Report:</u>
Feeling ambivalent about ending: sad, detached, relieved, withdrawn
<u>Graduating Students Report:</u>
Reappearance of self doubt
Being distracted by new demands - relocating, job search, license exam
<u>First-Year Students Report:</u>
Feeling ambivalent about ending: sad, detached, relieved, withdrawn
Looking forward with confidence to the next practicum
Having clearer expectations for the next practicum
Being concerned about meeting higher expectations for the next practicum

<u>Students Need:</u>
To reflect on past experiences with endings; identify patterns
To share feelings with seminar members and field instructor
To start the closure process early
To develop an ending plan
To reflect on their growth and learning
To use learning to develop new goals and future plans

LEARNING THROUGH FIELD

Stage One

Beginning

STUDENTS REPORT:

Feeling like a stranger, then a guest

Feeling vulnerable and self-conscious

Being enthusiastic about assignments, yet fearful

Feeling anxious about meeting other staff

Feeling overwhelmed

STUDENTS NEED:

- A safe place to share concerns with seminar members and faculty liaison
- Permission to be learners; to understand learning styles
- To build self-awareness of strengths and limitations
- To identify support systems
- To discuss feelings and questions with field instructor

  To be introduced at the agency, to have a place to sit, to leave coat, papers
- Clarification of roles, expectations, and policies

  A written orientation plan

  A plan to focus goals and meet general requirements

  To individualize placement

  To understand how to use supervision in planning and reviewing work

  Skills to start work assignments

- **Indicates a focus of this chapter**

2

Chapter One

Preparing to Learn

Why do we do field?
All that work and no pay?!
What can I expect from field?
What if I make a mistake?
How do I know what I need?
But I've done all this before!

VIGNETTES

Lucia walks slowly into the seminar room, taking in as much as possible while still looking nonchalant and, she hopes, calm. Some faces look familiar from last week's Student Orientation, but none of their names surface in her mind. Evident in front of each student is the Field Education Manual. Lucia tried to read this last night but found herself too distracted, excited, and worried. She wracked her brain trying to remember material that had been covered in the handful of social work classes she'd taken and wondered if she could remember to use it. Lucia took a deep breath and let it out as a sigh. With normal classes you knew what was coming: readings, discussions, tests, papers. But field was different.

George sits down next to Lucia. His practicum is at the East Neighborhood Center. He'll start tomorrow and knows he will like it. He really hit it off well with the kids and his field instructor during his interview. But he was totally unprepared for a question from his field instructor: How do you think your being an African American man will affect your ability to work with the twelve- to thirteen-year-old Hmong girls that will be in your after-school group? Should he have talked about the diverse neighborhood where he lives? About his loving relationship with his own little sister? Should he talk with his field instructor about being gay? What should he tell his seminar members? And he thought he was prepared for field!

Saleema is in the seminar, too. She knows exactly what she wants and knows she will be comfortable in her practicum. She used to be an elementary school teacher and has known since last spring that she will be in an elementary school setting this year. She hopes they don't consider her "just a student"; she's got a lot to offer them. She wonders what her students will call her and if she will have a "field" classroom of her own or even a desk.

DEVELOPMENTAL FEATURES

Most students are anxious when they start field. As in any new experience, we each react differently; those who are introverted tend to be more nervous about meeting people; those who need to feel a sense of control need as much concrete information as possible; those who like change and excitement may not be anxious until later. Often in the first few days when students begin field, they feel like a stranger - they don't know the staff or what to expect. Like Saleema, they need to know if they will have a desk, what people will call them, and where the bathroom is. Since the relationship with the field instructor is so critical, students like George often are unsure what to discuss and what not to mention yet. A seminar with other students in field is usually a vital and reassuring component, but that first meeting, for students like Lucia, can be daunting. Some students are not sure social work is a good fit for them and others are not quite sure what field is and how it relates to what is taught in class.

It is helpful for all types of students to know what lies ahead. This chapter will help to set the stage for beginning your practicum.

INTEGRATION AND APPLICATION

So much of what humans learn to do is the result of numerous individual tasks integrated into a complex whole. Even mundane daily activities, like driving a car, involve the integration of multiple bits of knowledge and skill. How did we ever learn to steer, accelerate, watch ahead of us, to the side of us, and in two or three mirrors, all the while navigating, imagining the dangerous whims of other drivers, reading the road signs, adjusting the radio, and convincing our child to stay in the car seat?! When we are able to do these individual tasks almost automatically, our learning has become integrated through direct application and practice.

Learning the practice of professional social work is an infinitely more complex challenge that involves the work of a lifetime. Starting as students we begin collecting the foundation of knowledge and theory, a repertoire of skills and methods, and an understanding of and commitment to values and ethics that will guide our work. Social work, since its beginning, has educated students not only with books, in classrooms and labs, but in the actual settings where working with people happens. Education for social work practice requires the intense and interpersonal experiences we can only find in real agencies and organizations, with real people, and with the focused one-to-one mentorship that can be provided by a field instructor.

Many students are attracted to social work in part because they enjoy and learn well by "doing." For them the challenge is often to remember and utilize the theories and knowledge they are learning in the traditional classroom. For other students, the theoretical learning is easy, but face-to-face exchanges are intimidating. Field education gives students the valuable opportunity to identify competencies, perspectives, and values that are useful in all social work settings, to see how practitioners develop under supervision, to imagine themselves in this particular area of practice with these specific client groups, and to determine if social work itself is a good "fit" for their interests and abilities. While dealing with these challenges, students are engaged simultaneously in learning how this particular agency or organization functions, what diverse groups it serves, how it interacts with communities, other agencies, regulatory bodies and policy makers, and what the role of a social worker is in all this mix.

As you enter the world of field education, we encourage you to remember that it is a complex learning process, that some areas will be more challenging than others and that eventually many tasks will become as automatic as driving a car. Most students feel anxious when faced with new beginnings, but find that confidence and competence grow as the practicum unfolds.

WHAT IS FIELD?

Let's discuss for a moment what field is not. Field is not employment, though the two experiences are similar.   The primary focus of an employed position is dictated by the organization's mission.   The organization contracts with employees to perform certain tasks or functions in order to meet their mission.   A field placement is not a volunteer position, either. Like employees, volunteers contract individually with the agency to meet the agency goals, and not primarily the volunteers' needs. Volunteers are expected to fulfill roles as adjuncts to paid staff, to complement and augment the tasks assigned to professionals. While some students utilize places of employment as field placements, or have volunteer experience with the agency they select, it is imperative to clarify the differences in the roles of student and employee or volunteer. Separating these roles will help assure that you, as a student, are not short-changed in your field experience.   For further discussion of issues related to practicum in place of employment, please refer to Appendix D.

Unlike paid positions or volunteer programs, a field program is a joint venture of the social work program, the agency, and the student. Each member of this triad must work together to assure that goals are harmonious. An accredited social work program is accountable to the national Council on Social Work Education (CSWE) to provide a quality program that prepares students for professional social work practice. The program must demonstrate that it has clear objectives for this field requirement. It must show that it utilizes consistent criteria for the recruitment of both agency sites and agency field instructors, and it must explain the learning expectations of the students. Faculty or staff from the social work program have responsibilities to oversee the placement to assure that these standards are met.

The agency selected as a field placement site understands that the practicum is an educational program, a valuable aspect of preparing future professionals. The agency has reviewed its programs and staff to determine whether it can meet the educational requirements of the college or university and has designated a person in the agency to devote time and energy to the student's education.

This learning-centered model has two important implications. First, students must be focused actively on their learning: to be aware of and responsive to their learning needs, to advocate for those needs, and to be open to feedback about their learning styles and barriers. Second, students are training for professional positions and are expected to take continual steps toward that role. Increasingly, they are expected to perform with professional accountability, practice professional ethics, utilize professional skills, and apply professional knowledge.

Field is not, then, volunteering or employment. In many respects, field is more challenging than a volunteer position because the expectations are generally higher and the stakes for the student's future are more important. There are many obligations tied to a pay check which students do not have. Students have instead the freedom to admit that they are learners, to try out a setting, to focus on their own professional developmental needs, and to engage the support of faculty and agency personnel to meet these needs.

WHAT TO EXPECT FROM OTHERS

For most of us, knowing ahead of time what to expect from a new experience helps us to prepare ourselves for it both emotionally and practically. Because of CSWE standards, all accredited social work programs will have some common features. The first thing to expect of your field education program, however, is that it will be, in some ways, unique. It has been tailored in response to the emphasis of the college or university's social work program and the decisions it has made in designing the curriculum as a whole, the style of the field program administration, the level of education you are pursuing, and the nature and needs of the agencies and organizations in your geographical area. Ask "Why do we do it this way?" to begin to understand the reasons behind the processes and policies your school has developed. Regardless of these differences, we can anticipate that field programs share many common expectations for the different facets or components working together in them.

The College or University Field Program

Each school has its own names for the players in field: students may be called interns or learners;   the agency-based practitioner may be called a practicum instructor, field instructor, agency instructor, or agency supervisor; and faculty may be called practicum liaisons, faculty liaisons, or field faculty supervisors. We will use the terms **"student"** (you), **"field instructor"** (to represent the agency-based person), and **"faculty liaison"** (representing the school). Please become familiar with your school's players and what they are called.

Your social work program will most likely assign a faculty liaison to work with students and agencies to coordinate field placements. Determine what the faculty's specific role is in your program in order to understand how you can best work with them during your practicum.

- Expect the faculty liaison to be committed to the quality of your practicum experience from beginning to end—to listen to your questions, advocate for your learning, work to understand your difficulties, and celebrate your successes. A faculty liaison usually implements the program's policies and requirements for field education and can be the person you turn to when questions or difficulties arise. Expect that field policies will be applied fairly and consistently and that a process will be provided for you to discuss decisions with which you might disagree.

' Expect your social work program to detail the specific goals and expectations they have for your learning and performance in your placement. Look for these in orientation materials or manuals. Expect your program to communicate with the agency in which you are placed so that field requirements are clear to all.

The Agency and Field Instructor

- Expect the field instructor to support you during a period of orientation, to work with you to design a learning contract, and to help you connect with other people in the agency from whom you can also learn.

- Expect regular supervision throughout your placement, clear expectations and assignments, and helpful feedback about all aspects of your professional performance. When difficulties arise, expect agency personnel to treat you respectfully.

- Expect the agency to provide material and training so that you are able to inform yourself about agency policies and perform assigned tasks within those guidelines. Expect the agency to support ethical behavior in harmony with social work values.

- Expect the agency to work with you to complete the necessary paperwork for the college or university that documents how you have met requirements and evaluates your performance.

Your Peers

Most field programs involve some aspect of group learning in which you are able to share your experiences and questions with other students and to learn by hearing about their agencies and experiences.

- Expect your peers to listen respectfully to you, to engage with you in problem solving as you encounter difficulties, and to identify and celebrate your progress. Expect that they will also be utilizing your experiences to learn for themselves.

- Expect your peers to bring to your group their own questions and experiences for discussion so that you can also provide your support and feedback and learn from their unique experiences.

- Expect your peers to be active group members in enforcing the norms of your group about equally sharing time and attention, working on relevant topics, respecting confidentiality, and keeping other group agreements.

- Expect your peers to be supportive, and expect that increasingly your group members will be able to provide each other with realistic feedback to assist in handling professional situations more constructively.

WHAT TO EXPECT FROM YOURSELF

We have discussed the multiple and complex goals of field and what to expect from your program and faculty, agency, and peers. You must also reflect on what to expect from yourself, the learner.

Expect to Feel Vulnerable.
Most students vacillate between feeling confident about what they already know and feeling fearful that they actually know less than they hope - and maybe less than others assume they know. This roller coaster of feelings is normal, but difficult and often emotionally exhausting. Remembering what you already know and celebrating how far you have come are good ways to handle the fear

and frustration often inherent in the student role. Many students arrive in social work programs with years of experience in related fields or in paraprofessional positions, or with advanced knowledge regarding certain populations and issues. The Council on Social Work Education (CSWE) does not allow social work programs to give credit for previous work experience, so you may worry that you will be wasting your time in your practicum. Whether you are worried that you may be in over your head or just wasting your time, the best preparation for a good practicum experience is cultivating a positive attitude that you can and will benefit from being a learner.

Expect to Build on Your Strengths.

We have just discussed feeling vulnerable. It is important, however, to ground our self-knowledge firmly in our strengths, for they help us not only discern what we can best accomplish, but will also ensure that we enjoy and thrive on our work. Our strengths are also pointers toward how to best handle those barriers and limitations we inevitably encounter.   Saleeby (1992) asserts:

> Individuals and groups have vast, often untapped and frequently unappreciated reservoirs of physical, emotional, cognitive, interpersonal, social, and spiritual energies, resources, and competencies. These are invaluable in constructing the possibility of change, transformation, and hope. It is clear that individuals sometimes do not define some of their attributes or experiences as resources. It is likewise true that individuals sometimes are unaware of some of their own strengths, that some of their knowledge, talents, and experience can be used in the service of recovery and development - their own and that of others. (p. 6)

Just as social work practice must begin by identifying and respecting the strengths and resources of an individual, family, or community, social workers must do no less for themselves. Unique cultural and personal differences must be considered when identifying strengths. Knowledge of your strengths can motivate you; when the going gets rough it feels much better to focus on your abilities and progress. Keeping your strengths in mind helps you to look honestly at your limitations and mistakes and keep them in perspective, avoiding a plunge into feelings of remorse and worthlessness. Your strengths may suggest ways you might collaborate with supervisors, instructors, and colleagues toward meeting your learning goals. Appreciation of your differences can help you avoid feeling like a victim when those differences become the focus of attention, or even blame. Finally, human strengths exist in a social, cultural, and spiritual context. Discovering what they are can lead you to resources in your own environment that you can use throughout your practicum - and your career.

Expect to Be a Learner.

While it is obvious that students are learners, in field, being "just a student" can be especially difficult if people assume you know nothing and are unaware of your strengths. It is also difficult if you have been successful at other jobs and careers before deciding to become a social worker. Saleema, in the vignette, has experience that will help her to be comfortable around children and in the school setting, but will still need to learn more about the social work role and perspective. Some students overcompensate and pretend to know everything; others act totally helpless. Whatever your background, remember that the goal is to build on your past experiences. Your own attitude will make an enormous difference in your approach to learning and your relationships with those involved in learning with you.

<u>Expect to explore your learning style.</u> Another aspect of self-awareness is knowing the way in which you best learn. Your learning style can be a strength, can point to what situations might prove challenging for you, and can help you to explain what you need from an agency and field instructor. If you have not completed a learning inventory, we suggest that you do so. Additional readings about learning styles are listed at the end of the chapter. You will need to communicate this information to your faculty and agency field instructor - do not expect that they

can guess your learning needs. When you are uncomfortable, not ready for some task, bored, wanting more responsibilities, needing a different style of learning or supervision, it is your responsibility to share this information. If you are having difficulty learning, it may be because you are not using your natural style, or you are using your preferred style so exclusively that there is not room to see and use other strategies when appropriate.

Expect to learn from others. Consider all those you work with as your teachers: Seek out their wisdom, listen to their stories, and observe how they interact with their environments. The clients, groups, and communities we work with teach us about diversity and resilience. Lessons learned from clients will be both rewarding and painful as we learn to connect, to work together, and to say good-bye.

Agency staff, volunteers, and field instructors teach us as we discuss issues, watch their work, and request their input on our performance. Field students often feel exposed since much of their work is public, is sometimes observed, and is always evaluated. Therefore, a strong and honest supervisory relationship with your field instructor is a key ingredient in successful field learning. Like all relationships, this is a two-way street. Understanding supervision and using it well can mean the difference between a good field placement and an excellent one.

Expect to learn "professional use of self." Social work education, and field work especially, require us to learn how to use ourselves. Valuing differences and bringing personal strengths into relationships and practice is an intentional process. One of the most challenging aspects of practice is discovering how to pay attention to our emotions, values, skills, and limitations, and to use these purposefully in work with others. Similarly challenging is knowing our individual blind spots and barriers, recognizing when our personal issues interfere with effective practice, and learning how to manage these situations.

Expect to learn appropriate boundaries. The issue of boundaries in social work practice is complex. Students often encounter the issue first as they struggle, as George did, with what to discuss with their field instructor. George has a variety of issues he considers disclosing which may help build the relationship with his field instructor. He will probably feel safe discussing his neighborhood sooner than he will feel safe disclosing that he is gay. Throughout your practicum, expect to struggle with why, when, and with whom to disclose personal issues and discuss differences. Related boundary issues you are likely to encounter - such as personal safety, transference, and the difference between therapy and supervision - will be discussed in later chapters.

<u>Expect to learn from mistakes.</u> In a classroom setting, we often expect to measure our learning by how few errors we make on exams. Getting it right the first time means a good grade and a feeling of mastery. Field can be especially intimidating because we can expect <u>not</u> to get it "right" the first time. If we wait to act until we have all the information and skills we need, we will be waiting a long time to do anything. Only by "doing it" can we engage in the very process that provides necessary information and skills. You and your field instructor in the agency will work together to decide what level of responsibilities you are ready for at a given time, but most field experiences involve some form of "jumping in" to test yourself and try out a new role, answer a question, or respond to a situation. Begin now to make a commitment to yourself to allow yourself to "fail" in order to learn what you'll never learn by playing it safe.

<u>Expect to learn from successes.</u> So far, we have urged you, in your student role, to identify what you don't know, to pay attention to your feelings, to seek out others' opinions of you, and to take risks beyond your comfort zone in order to learn. No wonder field can provoke anxiety! It is important also to remember that we learn by our successes as much as by our mistakes. Pay attention to your progress over time and notice even the small steps you are taking. When you ask for feedback, make sure you come away with ideas about how you are on the right track, how you have improved, and what concrete steps you

can take to continue growing. Make sure that you identify those people in your agency and at school who will provide you with support and encouragement. Learn to celebrate as you develop during the unique learning that we call field education.

JOURNAL ASSIGNMENTS:

1.1   Preparing an Inventory of Personal Strengths

List at least ten personal strengths that you will use and develop in your professional life. Compare your list with Table 1.1, "Check Out Your Fit with Social Work." Plan to add to the list as the year progresses. This list may be helpful as you graduate, write your resume, and interview for jobs.

1.2   Identifying Support Systems

Prepare an eco-map showing your support systems. Using a large piece of paper, write your name in the center and draw a circle around it. Now add to your map the major people, groups, or organizations that currently provide you with support. Consider family, partner, roommate, friends, neighbors, church, temple or synagogue, and other groups or organizations. Place the names on the map either very close to your own circle (for those that provide the most constant or strongest support) to those farthest away (for those that provide inconsistent, intermittent, or limited support). After you have placed each system on the paper, circle each one to see them better. How well do these groups function for you? What kinds of gaps do you see? Did this exercise make you aware of an unrecognized source of support? As the year progresses, revisit the map and add or delete systems as they change.

1.3   Starting to Think about Personal Issues

Reflect on factors that may interfere with your ability to be an effective social worker. Think about pivotal events in your life, areas where you feel vulnerable, or sensitive issues you feel unsure about. As you progress through your practicum, be mindful about these or other issues, and discuss their impact on your practice with your faculty liaison or field instructor.

1.4 Identifying Learning Style

Tell a story about a time that you learned something—a new hobby, skill, or a challenging subject. Describe the experience of learning: how you approached it, what strategies you used, what was helpful, and what was not. What does this story reveal about you as a learner? What in the story is typical about your learning style? What is unique or important for you in learning?

Check Out Your Fit with Social Work
Table 1.1

1.   Are you genuinely interested in people of all kinds? Social workers respect and appreciate racial, economic, cultural, religious, sexual, and other differences. Prejudice does not fit with our values.

2.   Do you believe in the human potential for growth and change? Social workers maintain that everyone has inner strengths and the ability to change.

3.   Do you have patience, perseverance, and the ability to follow through? Social workers must be hard to discourage and always resourceful in seeking new ways to help.

4.   Do you enjoy working with people? Social workers need to work collaboratively with clients, colleagues, and other professionals.

5.   Are you interested in developing your "people skills"? While social work skills may seem simple—listening, asking questions, sharing information, etc.—these skills are refined through extensive self-awareness and feedback from others.

6.   Are you interested in your own personal growth and well-being? Social workers must be aware of their strengths, needs, and limitations, and how these affect their professional interactions.

7.   Do you think you can work effectively in complex and ambiguous situations requiring sound judgment? Social workers must pick out key items from the mounds of information provided by a client, apply theory and research, discover effective methods to help people move toward goals, and make difficult decisions based on the best information available.

8.   Are you willing to develop the skills and knowledge to handle uncomfortable and sometimes dangerous situations that many people prefer to avoid: mediating differences, diffusing conflict, confronting an unresponsive party, or advocating for ethical policies?

9.   Are you interested in using scientific methods to work with people? Social workers base their practice on established methods and use research to further their knowledge and improve their skills.

10. Are you interested in the larger picture? A social worker cares about the state of the nation and world, seeing each human situation in relationship to the whole community. Social workers are committed to working for better housing, safer communities, better health services, better schools, and better wages.

Source: Adapted with permission from *1996 BSW Student Handbook*. School of Social Work, College of St. Catherine/University of St. Thomas, St. Paul, MN

SEMINAR ACTIVITIES:

1.1   Using Ice Breakers

a. In the seminar group, each person takes turns introducing himself or herself by name and by answering these questions:

- What am I most excited about when I think of field?
- What am I most anxious about when I think of field?
- What do I do to relieve stress?

b.   Each group member creates a large name tag with this information:

Favorite Place on Earth	NAME	Favorite Hobby
Where I Was Born		A Unique Thing about Me

Discuss the information in dyads for a few minutes. Each person is then introduced to the larger group by his or her partner.

c.   Complete a name tag with your first, middle, and last name. Take turns describing to the group how you got your middle name.

d.   Using crayons (to take a playful tone), draw an animal you would choose to represent yourself. Explain briefly to the group what qualities this animal has that led you to choose it.

1.2   Creating a Safe Seminar Atmosphere

Remember a place where you once felt safe and happy. Imagine it in your mind and allow yourself to be there for a few moments, enjoying the way it looked, sounded, and felt. Briefly describe to the group one or two things that made this place so special. One person will compile a running list of the general qualities of a safe place. After everyone is finished, examine the list together:

Which of these qualities can this group create? What needs to be added to the list?

1.3   Discussing   Learning   Styles

Choose several questions from the journal exercise about learning styles. In groups of three or four, discuss your response to these questions. As you learn more about your style and those of your group members, talk together about how learning style will impact field experiences and relationships with field instructors.

REFERENCES:

Saleeby, D. (1992). *The strengths perspective in social work practice.* White Plains, NY: Longman.

Borup, J., & Herman, W.R. (1994). *Structuring orientation for field students and new employees.* Paper presented at Midwest Biennial CSWE, St. Paul, MN.

ADDITIONAL READINGS:

DiTiberio, J.K., & Hammer, A.L. (1993). *Introduction to type in college.* Palo Alto, CA: Consulting Psychologists Press, Inc.

Ginsberg, L.H. (1998). *Careers in social work.*   Boston: Allyn & Bacon.

Johnson, D.W. (1990). Self-disclosure. In *Reaching out: Interpersonal effectiveness and self-actualization* (4th ed.) (pp. 29-77). Englewood Cliffs, NJ: Prentice Hall.

Keirsey, D., & Bates, M. (1984). *Please understand me: Character and temperament types.* Del Mar, CA: Prometheus Nemesis.

Stage One

Beginning

STUDENTS REPORT:

Feeling like a stranger, then a guest

Feeling vulnerable and self-conscious

Being enthusiastic about assignments, yet fearful

Feeling anxious about meeting other staff

Feeling overwhelmed

STUDENTS NEED:

• A safe place to share concerns with seminar members and faculty liaison
• Permission to be learners; to understand learning styles
• To build self-awareness of strengths and limitations
  To identify support systems
• To discuss feelings and questions with field instructor
• To be introduced at the agency, to have a place to sit, to leave coat, papers
• Clarification of roles, expectations, and policies
• A written orientation plan
  A plan to focus goals and meet general requirements
  To individualize placement
  To understand how to use supervision in planning and reviewing work
  Skills to start work assignments

• **Indicates a focus of this chapter**

Chapter Two

Planning Your Orientation

What will happen on the first day?
What do I need to know?
How can I remember everything?
Will the agency staff accept me?

VIGNETTE

Joan was used to a rushed morning routine after fifteen years of office work, and thought her first day at the clinic would seem like old times. Noah complained of a stomach ache and refused to take his bag lunch when Joan insisted he go to school anyway. The traffic was better than she feared, however, and she arrived 30 minutes too early! After carefully touching up her makeup in the rearview mirror for twenty minutes, Joan went in and introduced herself to the receptionist. She got only a blank stare and was told to have a seat. Fifteen minutes passed. The magazines were old. Should she ask the receptionist again or would that seem rude? Were these people walking past her in jeans other clinic workers? Should she not have worn her best suit? Why was she feeling so intimidated after all her years of experience?

Suddenly her field instructor appeared, apologetic for being late, and led her into the staff room. Over a small desk crammed into the corner floated a balloon that read "WELCOME!" On top of the desk was a name tag "Joan Bernstein, Social Work Intern," a file folder, and several thick manuals. "I had hoped to spend the morning together, Joan, but this emergency has me tied up until after lunch. Here's some stuff to read and an outline of the orientation I've planned for you. I'll come get you at 1:00 and we'll discuss it. Oh, help yourself to coffee. Glad you're here!"

The orientation plan was mainly a list of people to talk to and staff meetings she would be attending - starting today at 2:00! Joan tried to look like she was reading the manuals, but she'd never learn all this stuff. People smiled when they came in for coffee but said nothing. Maybe she could go wandering the halls and see what was up - or would she get in the way? Maybe she should make more coffee? She picked up the phone but was unable to get an outside line to check on Noah. What would she do if it rang? As noon approached, two things began to dominate Joan's thoughts: Would this afternoon be better - or worse? And why was she going back to school anyway?

DEVELOPMENTAL FEATURES

Put yourself in Joan's place. What would feel the most awkward to you? What would you have appreciated? Would you read the manuals in peace, go find someone to talk to, or leave a note that your son was sick and go home? What would you be most eager to do? Most nervous about? If the field instructor checked in with you, what question would you ask?

Students universally recognize the feelings Joan experienced. The first day of a new field placement can entail all the excitement of a visit to a foreign country - the sights and sounds and even the language are new and interesting. You can feel, simultaneously, that you have nothing really to do, and yet be overwhelmed by options. Other people know you are a stranger. They may be polite, rude, or indifferent, but they will watch to see how well you handle yourself and how you react to the things they take for granted. This can all be thrillingly adventurous, but it lacks the comfort and predictability of your "home turf." You know in your gut that you do not belong, and you are not sure yet if you can even learn to fit in. Extra energy is required to observe carefully for cues on what is expected, navigate the unfamiliar territory, and monitor your own behavior to try to be a good guest: courteous, attentive, undemanding, and maybe even helpful.

In time, field placement students generally move toward feeling more at home: making connections, remembering basic information, and even setting up their own space. But more than just time is needed. The beginning phase is not just a difficult stage to get past so the real work can start. Beginnings <u>themselves</u> are important. When a field placement gets off to a good start, a foundation has been laid that will strengthen everything that follows. Students can move more smoothly into the agency's life, equipped with basic information that allows them to take on responsibilities with increased confidence. The agency, in turn, has become aware of the students and how they will be supervised. Most importantly, the student and the field instructor have clarified roles and expectations to establish a beginning working relationship. Within this relationship, the practicum can develop into its full learning potential.

The beginning phase of placement presents unique challenges and requires thoughtful planning and adequate time. This chapter's goals are to assist you in recognizing the importance of the first weeks in your placement and to better deal with them through a comprehensive orientation process.

THE VALUE OF PLANNED ORIENTATION

When Joan, in the vignette, thinks of orientation, she may remember the two-hour meeting she attended at her last job where the human resources staff discussed time cards, insurance, and the mission of the organization. Joan may have even had a short tour and met the director. When we talk in this book about orientation, however, we have in mind the process of becoming familiar with the role of a student in the agency and learning about that agency's staff, clients, and the community it serves. A two-hour meeting cannot possibly accomplish these goals. We believe orientation is a process that takes place over several weeks and perhaps months. Sometime during this period you will be developing a learning contract, which is discussed in the next chapter.

Some organizations and field instructors will have a plan for student orientation. However, some field settings are so chaotic or crisis-oriented that staff have never had the luxury to think through systematically how to introduce a newcomer to what they do. Others may not have ever had a student, or may not understand how important a thoughtful beginning can be. We outline and discuss a general orientation plan on three levels: micro, mezzo, and macro (Borrup & Herman, 1994). The plan which is shown in Table 2.1 is very detailed; you and your field instructor can adapt it for your agency. We suggest that you also keep a running list of questions you want to ask as your orientation progresses. You will not always be able to get answers as soon as the question occurs to you, so a list can help you to keep track of your questions until the appropriate time.

An orientation plan is, however, more than just a checklist of information to be covered. You will need to discuss, and even better, write down, the Five W's:

- **what** will be included in your orientation;
- **who** will be responsible for each step;
- **where** you will need to go to find the person, meeting, or material you need;
- **when** a particular piece should be completed; and
- **why** any orientation item whose relevance or importance is not clear to you is included.

MICRO LEVEL OF ORIENTATION

At the micro level of orientation, the student and field instructor need to discuss the meaning and mechanics of supervision and initiate the important work of developing their relationship. That relationship is complex. The field instructor is there to teach you, support you, evaluate you, and at the same time make sure the agency's clients are well served. As a student, you want to learn, yet be professional and not too dependent. You want to increase your self-awareness, yet not expose too much. You want to trust the field instructor, yet not be too vulnerable. As you begin this working relationship, we encourage you to be open, honest, and respectful with each other; it is important to discuss your developing relationship as well as tasks and details.

One way to handle details is to construct a written Beginning Agreement even before discussing the specifics of an orientation plan. Form 2.1, located at the end of the chapter, provides an example. This agreement formalizes some very basic arrangements, assuring that both of you start the placement in basic harmony.

A Beginning Agreement should clarify the overall goal for the practicum, keeping in mind the expectations of the social work program, student, field instructor, and agency. This goal will give direction to the rest of the orientation and the development of the learning contract. You and your field instructor will need to agree on a title such as "Student Social Worker." This can ease the introductions of your first weeks and help you honestly represent your role to clients and others. Your title helps distinguish you and your role from those of staff, volunteers, and students from other disciplines. The Beginning Agreement should also specify the general times you expect to be at the agency and determine your projected ending date. To plan meaningful assignments, your field instructor must know when you anticipate finishing your required hours. Usually, the details of scheduling and ending dates can be renegotiated if needed.

Your orientation plan must take into account how you learn. As we discussed in Chapter One, your learning style affects how you approach a new challenge. If you are the type that likes to sit back and watch, please discuss this with your field instructor. Your instructor, by contrast, could be the type to jump right in and may have expected you to be the same. Or, your learning style may be to jump in and your field instructor may have assumed you would prefer to spend a week alone with the policy and procedure manuals before doing anything else. Talk to your field instructor about the impact of your learning style on orientation. For example, in the vignette, if Joan had mentioned during her placement interview that she needed an overall orientation to the people and agency before information in manuals could be valuable to her, perhaps the morning could have been different. Being involved in the emergency

Orientation Plan
Table 2.1

Micro Level of Orientation

A. **Orientation Plan**
Checklist and Five W's
Beginning Agreement
Learning styles

B. **Supervision**
Supervisor role and style
Previous experiences with supervision
Weekly supervision times
Who sets agenda for supervision meetings
What is discussed in supervision
How to discuss goals, fears, issues, assignments

C. **Expectations for Professional Behavior**
Agency boundaries: What is acceptable
                              What is unacceptable
Time off for illness, holidays, tests

D. **Integrating class work with field**

Syllabi, texts, assignments

Mezzo Level of Orientation

A. **Purpose, function, and structure of the agency**
Mission
Governance
Policies

B. **Who's Who**
Organizational charts
Job descriptions
List of people to meet

C. **Clients/Consumers/Constituents**
Who they are
In what ways they are served
How they get connected
What is the process for intake-termination
Costs for services

D. **Where is everything?**
Tour of agency
Student's desk, phone, files, etc.
Copy machine
Lunch/break room (who eats with whom and are students welcome?)

E. **Information   Flow**
    Telephone
    Computer use/access/rcsource person
    Routing   material
    Mail/ in box
    Messages
    Meetings required
F. **How   to   document**
    When and where
    Confidentiality in documentation
    Jargon,   abbreviations
    How to keep statistics
    What forms are required
G. **Confidentiality**
    Consent for release of information
    Confidential and privileged information
    Legal requirements to report; other legal parameters
H. **Safety**
    In the office
    In the neighborhood
I. **Resources**
    For clients/consumers/ constituents
    For students
    Bibliography of important books and articles
    Internet   availability
    Library journal access
    Mileage   reimbursement
    Workshop additional learning opportunities

Macro   Level   of   Orientation

A. **The   Community**
    Map of the neighborhood
    History of the neighborhood
    Strengths of the community
    Major issues affecting clients/population
    Aspects of diversity in the community
    Leadership in community

B. **Social   Service   System**
    List of area agencies and organizations
    How your agency fits in with similar agencies elsewhere
    How your agency coordinates with other types of agencies
    Coordinating/networking bodies in the   community
    History/perceptions/strengths/limitations of agency in community
    Funding for agencies

C. **Social   Policy**
    Government mandates or sanctions
    Who's who in regulatory bodies
    Regulatory   processes
    Legislation affecting   clients/agency

sounded exciting to Joan, but if going with the field instructor was not possible, perhaps she could have shadowed another worker.

"Integrating class work with field" is in the micro level of the orientation plan so that you and your field instructor can talk about what you will be learning in class and relate it to your work in field. For some students, it is difficult to integrate field and class material; discussing with your field instructor the texts and assignments will help make the connection. It may also help to note when midterms, finals, and school breaks are due so that the impact of those demands can be considered.

MEZZO LEVEL OF ORIENTATION

Orientation on the mezzo level requires learning about the unit or department you will be working with, the role of social workers and other staff, and the mission of the agency. In the most concrete sense this involves the layout of the agency: where you sit, where you'll get messages, and how to get supplies. More complex aspects include the history and philosophy of the agency, as well as its organization, policies, and procedures. Where can you find all the information you need for this level of orientation? Ask for information the agency or organization uses with the public: brochures, annual reports, and sometimes even short films. Agencies also have collections of information they use internally such as policy and procedure manuals and information related to parent organizations or regulatory and licensing bodies.

Your field instructor may provide this material or ask you to talk with a support staff member. Even if you get this information from your field instructor, take some time early on to chat with support staff. They can often explain aspects of the agency you will want to know about. They can ease your transition to feeling a part of the agency by helping set up mail boxes, message systems, basic supplies, keys, and explaining phone, computer, and copier services with expertise. In addition, support staff often know everyone, and are readily available at most times. They can be great allies to answer questions and provide some types of information when your instructor is unavailable.

Obviously, one of the best ways to find out about the agency is by talking to staff, but most students get nervous about meeting the other people in the agency. Students may worry whether staff will welcome and help them, or resent the extra demands on their time. Talking with your field instructor about how you will meet and interact with the staff is important. Ask about which times are best for informal chats and how to set up more formal interviews. Attending meetings for the first time can also be intimidating. You will probably find it helpful to discuss ahead of time who will be in the meetings, what the purpose is, some of the dynamics of the group, and if you will be expected to speak. While initially scary, meetings are fairly easy to prepare for, and doing this preparation may decrease your anxiety and ease your entrance into the agency system.

When you are ready to learn about specific agency services you might be providing, ask if you could see client files, samples of completed case histories, summaries of group meetings, minutes of important meetings, outlines of public presentations, or samples of past projects. You will need to know what forms are required, how to document, and how confidential information is handled. Manuals may have this information, but it is usually advisable to review these critical details with your field instructor. In preparing for the work you will be doing, plan a step-by-step process that involves some reading, observation, teaming, and independent work when you are ready.

MACRO LEVEL OF ORIENTATION

The macro area of orientation can seem overwhelming. It usually extends beyond your day-to-day tasks, familiar people, and immediate surroundings. However, to really learn where and how your agency fits in and to practice social work on all levels, it is absolutely essential to learn about these larger systems.

Your agency exists in a community which helps to define its mission and services. This community may be geographic. Your agency may be the only women's shelter in a small town, or a social services office for a specific county. It may be a mental health clinic with a designated catchment area in a large city, or a settlement house with historic ties to a specific neighborhood. Get a map that you can keep with you, refer to often, and mark it up. Learn how and where you can feel safe in this community. Spend several hours walking or driving around to get the feel of living in this particular place.

However, your agency may serve a community that is not defined in geographic terms. Perhaps it provides services to physically disabled clients from a large region, or special medical care to children from several states. You may work with gay and lesbian teens in public schools anywhere in your metropolitan area, or Hispanic families throughout your state. In large agencies, you may have several communities to learn about: neighborhood children in after-school groups, elderly clients from a high-rise housing site, or families who have adopted children. Learning about some large agencies may take several months.

As you determine what communities your agency serves, listen for the stories that those communities bring. Ask about the neighborhood's history and its leaders, past and present. What challenges has it faced, and how did it organize to do so? What issues unite, and perhaps divide, the residents?

Social service agencies are a part of a community system. Most communities have a directory of social service agencies. You may also be able to consult specialized directories of resources for a particular age or ethnic group. Some communities have monthly meetings for representatives from local agencies that serve as a clearinghouse for information, and often plan and coordinate the community's service network. With whom does your own agency work most closely? How are the services coordinated and how are referrals made? How do your agency's mission, services, funding, or philosophy differ from others? How is the agency perceived in this larger system?

Finally, most agencies are accountable to some larger body for their use of funds and quality of services. Find out what governmental mandates or funding streams resulted in your programs. How does the agency keep tabs on legislation that affects its clientele, services, and funding? To whom does the administration report, and what types of reports are required? Are your agency services affiliated with or accredited by a national parent organization? If it is licensed by a regulatory body, how do the requirements affect how the agency operates? Are certain programs funded by grants from foundations, or are they being tested as pilots of new or innovative services?

The macro level of orientation provides information that helps you to set your agency or organization into a larger context. You begin to learn why specific policies exist and why documentation is important and how it is used. You are more easily able to see the lives of the people you work with in a holistic manner as you become familiar with the community's strengths and resources and challenges. This information does not just belong in manuals or in materials for boards of directors. This is information you can begin to put to use to understand, serve, and advocate for the people who use your agency or organization.

Only as you can begin see the big picture of your agency, including the micro, mezzo, and macro perspectives, can you effectively understand and learn to practice on all those levels as a social worker. A well-planned and thorough orientation can assist you through the difficult early period of a placement and ease you into the life of the agency. The wealth of information you collect during this period can be useful years later in your professional practice even in very different settings. The first use you will have for this information, however, will be to negotiate the specifics of what you will do during your practicum in order to better focus your learning.

JOURNAL ASSIGNMENTS:

2.1 Anticipating the First Day

Beginning at a practicum agency is a pivotal milestone in your professional career. Take the time the night before you begin at the agency to write about your feelings as you anticipate tomorrow. At the end of your first day, write about all the events and the feelings you experienced. How do you feel about yourself and your choice of a social work career after this first day? This record could be a valuable keepsake!

2.2 Revisiting Learning Style

Revisit your learning style reflections in Chapter One. As you progress in orientation, what are you discovering about your learning style? These insights can be useful to record for your next orientation period at another practicum or in employment.

2.3 Thinking about Supervision

Reflect on your relationship with your supervisor in these first weeks. What is working well? What is uncomfortable? Identify any issues you would like to discuss with your faculty liaison or seminar members.

2.4 Reflecting on Seminar Participation

Take time soon after your field seminar meeting to write reflections about your group experience and participation. What did you learn about social work? What was your participation like? What did you learn about yourself? How well is your group working? In what ways would you like to improve your group participation? We suggest repeating this exercise monthly.

SEMINAR ACTIVITIES:

2.1 Discussing Your First Day

After your first day, share with seminar members what was the most exciting and the most anxiety-producing experience at the agency and your responses to those events.

2.2 Checking In

Each student responds to these questions during check-in:
- What's the most challenging or difficult thing that has happened at my practicum since the last meeting?
- What's the most exciting or enjoyable thing?
- What one insight have I gotten related to social work issues?

(This is a good way to start each seminar.)

2.3 Making an Agency Presentation

When you have had a chance to learn about your agency, make an informal presentation to your seminar about the agency. This will help you understand the agency better and help your seminar colleagues learn about another resource. Form 2.2 provides an example of an Agency Presentation Outline.

BEGINNING AGREEMENT
Form   2.1

Name of Student: _____

Name of Agency: _____

Field Instructor Name: _____

Student's Placement Title: _____

Overall goal for this placement:

_____

_____

_____

_____

Briefly describe the plan for orientation to this agency:

_____

_____

_____

Approximate numbers of hours per week in fieldwork agency: _____

Beginning date of Fieldwork: _____

Expected completion date of Fieldwork: _____

_____

Student's Signature

_____

Field Instructor's Signature

_____   _____

Faculty Liaison's Signature   Date

AGENCY PRESENTATION OUTLINE
Form 2.2

1.   Name of agency:

2.   Brief history of agency:

3.   At least three major goals or purposes of the agency:

4.   Source of the agency's funding:

5.   Organizational structure of the agency:

Governing body:

Administrative staff:

Direct staff:

Where do the social services fit in the structure?:

6.   Community served:
What types of diversity exist among those populations served?

7.   Brief description of the agency's major programs or services:

8.   Role of the social worker in this agency:

REFERENCE:

Borrup, J., & Herman, W.R. (1994). *Structuring orientation for field students and new employees.* Paper presented at Midwest Biennial CSWE, St. Paul, MN.

ADDITIONAL READINGS:

Berger, S.S., & Bucholz, E.S. (1993). On becoming a supervisee: Preparing for learning. *Psychotherapy, 30,* 86-92.

Bogo, M. (1993). The student/field instructor relationship: The critical factor in field education. *The Clinical Supervisor, 11,* 23-36.

Chuck, F. (1995, Fall). Preparing for supervision. *The New Social Worker,* 8-9.

Inglehart, A.P., & Becerra, R.M. (1995). *Social services and the ethnic community.* Boston: Allyn & Bacon.

Netting, F.E., Erlish, J.L., & McMurtry, S.L. (1993). Framework for analyzing a human service organization. In *Social work macro practice* (pp. 192-197). New York: Longman.

Verson, G. (1995). Be careful, it's a jungle out there: A look at risks in field placement. *The New Social Worker, 2*(1), 7-8.

Stage One

Beginning

STUDENTS REPORT:

Feeling like a stranger, then a guest

Feeling vulnerable and self-conscious

Being enthusiastic about assignments, yet fearful

Feeling anxious about meeting other staff

Feeling overwhelmed

STUDENTS NEED:

A safe place to share concerns with seminar members and faculty liaison

• Permission to be learners; to understand learning styles

To build self-awareness of strengths and limitations

To identify support systems

• To discuss feelings and questions with field instructor

To be introduced at the agency, to have a place to sit, to leave coat, papers

• Clarification of roles, expectations, and policies

A written orientation plan

• A plan to focus goals and meet general requirements

• To individualize placement

To understand how to use supervision in planning and reviewing work

Skills to start work assignments

• **Indicates a focus of this chapter**

40

Chapter Three

Focusing Your Learning

There's so much - I'm so excited!
There's not enough - I'm so bored!
What do social workers really do here?
I'm not sure I can work with old people.
I get it, but I don't really like it.

VIGNETTES

Tan has begun working in the food shelf at the community center. A Hmong family comes in who do not speak English, so his field instructor asks him to interpret. When Tan asks where they live, he remembers from reading about the food shelf program that this family does not live in the geographical area covered. Tan explains that they cannot be served at this site. The family is very angry with him.

Trish's placement is at the juvenile treatment center. The clients' ages range from fifteen to eighteen. The guys whistle at her and make remarks. This has been going on for a week, and although she has asks them to stop, they don't.

Alfred is at an elementary school. He is very excited to be working with the kids and can't wait to deal with the issues he will have on his caseload: the third-grade boy who has a diagnosis of ADHD; the kindergartner who came in today with a bruised face, whose teacher is concerned about possible abuse; and the sixth grader who is the class bully, who was referred for fighting on the bus. Wow.

Carlos is at a crisis line waiting for his first call. Nothing happens all afternoon. Though two calls come in that evening, three other people are working.

Alice's placement is a transitional housing program. Today, one social worker is only taking a client to the doctor and then helping her find furniture. The other social worker just filled out forms so she could get information from a client's previous worker, and is now making a million phone calls to locate a treatment program for the client and child care for the three girls while their mother is in treatment.

DEVELOPMENTAL FEATURES

As students pass through the first developmental stage of field placement, the early anxiety may begin to change. Orientation can assist students to feel more comfortable with the people, places, and services at the agency. As they feel more comfortable, they may become more excited about the time they will spend there and the skills they can learn. On the other hand, as the newness wears off, some students begin to question whether their placement will be right for them. In either case, students usually become somewhat overwhelmed as their knowledge of the agency builds and they begin confronting the task of creating a useful practicum experience from the possibilities and realities they have discovered.

Perhaps, like Alfred, you see each day filling up with challenges; but maybe, like Carlos, you are a bit bored at this point. If your experience is similar to Alice's, you may wonder if you are going to school for a career in finding furniture and babysitters! Like Tan and Trish, you may find some aspects of your placement distressing or distasteful. Your practicum requires active and concerted planning and designing. How can you go about shaping your time and activities so that you learn the most you can during your field placement? We suggest a two-step process to focusing your practicum:

- **Assess** - the possibilities, the challenges, the requirements
- **Plan** - the goals you will set, the strategies to meet them, and the ways to monitor your learning.

ASSESS

- **Program requirements**
- **Agency possibilities**
- **Personal needs**

Assess Program Requirements

By the time you are ready to focus your learning in the field placement, you will be familiar with what is required by your social work program, and connected with persons who can help you to understand and interpret those requirements in your specific placement. Does your school offer a set of general goals or a structured contract to complete? What kinds of experiences are recommended or required for field students in your program? Beginning your assessment with this information will help keep the focus on <u>learning</u> and on your role as a social work <u>student</u>. Alice's social work program, for example, requires her to complete a case management plan with a client. In doing this, she will discover the importance of community networking and referrals. Carlos will be required to complete a research project. Tan is required to work with people from a different cultural group.

Assess Agency Possibilities

The information you have gained during agency orientation will also be valuable. The basic information about how the agency works on micro, mezzo, and macro levels describes the spectrum of services and activities in which you may participate. Take Carlos, for example. In his orientation he learned the basics of crisis counseling and the processes followed by the crisis workers. He was informed that weekends and holidays are very busy for the phone lines; he has experienced that weekdays can be very slow. Carlos was also introduced to workers in the community education program who provide public presentations to school children on mental health issues. He became familiar with the organizational structure of the agency, which includes a board of directors and several committees made up of staff and volunteers. He learned that the neighborhood has a new population of refugees from Somalia. As Carlos begins to assess how to shape his practicum, he has a lot of useful information. He might explore changing his days on the crisis line to weekends; perhaps he could also work with the community education program, join a committee, or gather information about Somalians. In addition, Carlos will need to work with his field instructor to determine which of these responsibilities the agency is willing for a student to take. He will need to consult with his faculty liaison to match his interests with the program's requirements.

Assess Personal Needs

Self-awareness of your own strengths, personal issues, limitations, and goals is a third facet of this assessment process. (Refer back to assignments in Chapter One.) Your learning contract should allow you to build on strengths, address personal issues that affect practice, and increase your knowledge and skills in working with unfamiliar issues or populations. Trish believes that assertiveness is one of her strengths, but she is unsure how to use that skill with the teens without alienating them. She is also aware that her assertiveness may be perceived differently by the American Indian population at the center. Refer to the sample of her learning contract in Table 3.1 for how she might address these learning needs.

Tan will also use his self-awareness to build a learning contract. After his experience in the food shelf, Tan discussed with his field instructor how confrontation is a difficult and somewhat foreign concept to him. They agreed that this might be one of the goals for his field contract. His field instructor also noted that asking him to translate had put Tan in an awkward position. Tan revealed, then, that he was unsure how he will function as a professional within his small Hmong community. His field instructor suggested that he may want to interview other Hmong professionals to explore further what being a social worker might be like for him.

Assessing what your program requires, what your agency offers, and what is especially meaningful to you will help begin

LEARNING CONTRACT
Table 3.1

Name: Trish Murphy   Field Instructor: John Crowfoot

Agency: Sky County Juvenile Treatment Center

GOAL	STRATEGIES	EVALUATION
Micro		
1. Improve family interviewing skills	Observe 4-6 workers behind 1-way glass	Interview each worker on style & discuss with John
	Complete intakes with John until November.	Get feedback from John
		Complete 2 process recordings or video tapes by March
2. Learn how to develop and implement individual treatment plan	Be responsible for caseload of 6-8 residents by Jan. 1st	Draft treatment plans for John to review before case staffing
		Prepare update on each case for weekly supervision
3. Become more comfortable with my authority & role	Read Your Perfect Right	Write in my journal about my reactions to boys' remarks & discuss with John and Sarah
	Interview Sarah about handling boys' remarks	
	Implement ideas for decreasing remarks	

GOAL	STRATEGIES	EVALUATION
Mezzo		
4. Learn juvenile court processes	Attend court on 3rd Tues. each month	
	Interview Judge Whipple	Get John's feedback on proposed questions & discuss interview afterwards
	Prepare a Student Guide to court for agency	Draft to John by Feb. 1; final version to internship director by April 30
5. Become familiar with referral resources	Visit Family Outreach Services & Indian Family Center	Update resource file by May 1st
	Attend Sky Co. Social Service Association meetings at least twice	Prepare Community Profile assignment for seminar
Macro		
6. Become familiar with legislative & social action	Attend committee meeting on House Bill # 4022 reforming sentencing process	Give oral report to Center staff
	Participate in Prevent Violence taskforce	Incorporate learning in policy paper
7. Improve knowledge of American Indian culture	Interview social worker at reservation	Share Culture Presentation for Practice class with staff
	Read professional journal article on American Indian culture and social work practice	Discuss with John

the process of focusing your time and energy at the field placement. The connections you have made within your agency and social work program will be good resources to help determine what is especially interesting and what is especially challenging for you at this specific placement.

PLANNING A LEARNING CONTRACT

- **Develop a Learning Contract that is clearly designed.**
- **Develop a Learning Contract that is well-balanced.**

After assessing your field situation, you and your field instructor will need to select specific responsibilities and tasks for your placement. We recommend formalizing this plan in an individualized learning contract to be signed by both the field instructor and the faculty liaison. A learning contract provides the overall structure for the placement, clarifies the expectations of all involved, makes evaluations easier, and eventually provides a record of what you completed in this placement. Such a contract should be considered a working document, subject to review and revision as a part of ongoing supervisory conferences.

Formulating a learning contract is a complex task, and we strongly encourage you to involve your field instructor and faculty liaison throughout the process. You might ask to see copies of contracts previous students have written. Plan to sketch out drafts, ask for feedback, and make several revisions along the way. Often a face-to-face conference with your field instructor, faculty liaison, and you is helpful to clarify, refine, and finalize the document. In order to provide a working plan, your contract needs to be clearly designed and well balanced.

A Good Learning Contract Is Clearly Designed.

In order to be an effective tool for focusing on the educational objectives of field education, a student's learning contract should include the following components:

GOALS - what you hope to achieve
STRATEGIES - the work you will do to reach those goals
EVALUATION - ways to determine how well those strategies
   are addressing your goals and how well you have met
   those goals

Understanding the purpose of each of these three components can help you to design each one carefully. Alice, in this chapter's vignette, realizes that she does not understand what the social workers in the housing program are doing. They seem to be swamped with disconnected and trivial tasks, yet appear to find their positions meaningful and often describe this as "real social work." One of Alice's goals is to understand the role of the social worker in housing programs. These are her ideas for strategies to reach that goal:

1. *Manage a caseload of 4-6 clients*
2. *Participate in agency staff conferences each week where client service plans are reviewed by multidisciplinary team*
3. *Complete intake process and case management plan with at least two new clients*
4. *Interview 3 social workers in similar agencies by March 1: the homeless shelter, the independent teen living program, and the housing coordinator at the AIDS Project.*

Alice will also need to determine how well these strategies work to meet her goal and how well she carried out the strategies. Both types of evaluation are necessary to identify her learning in the placement. For "Manage a caseload," for instance, Alice can plan to evaluate her learning by keeping case notes which will be reviewed by her field instructor, reporting about her work with cases during each supervisory conference, and presenting one case in her field seminar. Refer to material from research courses for other ideas on how to evaluate your practice.

You can see from this example that a clearly designed contract:

- differentiates between goals, strategies, and evaluation;
- has goals that are concrete, specific, and measurable;
- has strategies that spell out the student's responsibilities, specifying how many, how often, by when, etc.;
- shows how the student and field instructor will work together to evaluate the student's responsibilities, performance, and learning; and
- designs evaluation procedures that involve opportunities for the field instructor to give student regular feedback to improve performance.

A Good Learning Contract Is Well Balanced.

Along with clearly designing the individual components of a learning contract, you must also check whether the contract as a whole provides a well-balanced plan. You have already assessed your program's requirements, your agency's possibilities, and your individual needs. Check for balance both within these categories and between the categories themselves.

For example, Alfred, in the vignette, is obviously excited about working individually with the wide variety of children in his school. The school and field instructor badly need his help with the many crises that erupt daily. If Alfred's learning contract refers only to working with individual children, however, he will have missed many opportunities for other types of learning.

Your social work program may have requirements that must be included in your learning contract. You may be expected to develop goals to improve skills in working with diverse populations or to have responsibilities on micro, mezzo, and macro levels of practice. Alfred's program may require him to visit another agency during his placement, or to complete a project involving research or social action. Many field requirements are designed to assure that each placement helps prepare students for a variety of fields of practice and agency types. Your faculty liaison is a resource person to make sure that your plans meet the school's requirements.

Your field instructor is the expert on what social work activities are central to the agency, which are possible for you to be involved in, and what level of responsibility would be appropriate. Alfred's field instructor, for example, indicated that he ought to gain experience in leading groups at the school, and suggested that he co-facilitate a friendship group the first semester, then lead a second-semester group on his own. Check your contract for balance between:

> Types of tasks: Balance caseload responsibilities with reading; balance working alone and working with other staff; balance understanding the agency with learning about the community.
>
> Levels of responsibility: As the placement progresses you should plan for your autonomy to increase. Continue working on tasks that have become comfortable for you as well as adding new ones that may be more challenging and stressful.
>
> Types of evaluation: Use variety, including informal notes or reflections for discussion, written reports, verbal feedback, direct observation, and audio or video tapes.

Personal needs should also have a balanced presence in a learning contract. Personal goals should stretch you, but they should not all center on your most vulnerable areas. Perhaps Alfred knows that time management is a big issue for him. He takes a risk when he formulates a goal to be on time, keep a calendar, and learn to prioritize tasks. For another personal goal, however, he may want to choose something less risky for him, perhaps to become more comfortable working with physically disabled children.

Finally, learning contracts should also have a balance <u>between</u> these three major areas. The program managers need to see that you are responsive to their requirements. The field instructor needs to feel that you are committed to learning the unique work and perspective of the agency. And finally, in setting appropriate personal learning goals, you need to demonstrate self-awareness and an ability to take risks.

Feeling overwhelmed is a good signal that the time has come to construct a learning contract. After you assess what is required, what is possible in the agency, and what your personal needs include, you can develop a clear and balanced contract that will map out the directions your practicum will take. The very process of writing a learning contract also builds the relationships among you, the field instructor, and faculty liaison. Since it is not written in stone, but will need to be revisited regularly, a learning contract provides an important tool to focus learning throughout your practicum.

JOURNAL ASSIGNMENTS:

3.1 Addressing Strengths and Vulnerabilities
Refer to Journal Assignments 1.1 and 1.3. Reflect on how your personal strengths and vulnerabilities can be addressed in this practicum.

3.2 Thinking about a Learning Contract
Use your journal to prepare your thoughts before drafting a learning contract. Make lists as you assess the possibilities, challenges, and requirements of your placement. Which do you feel most excited about? Which are going to be hardest for you to handle?

SEMINAR ACTIVITIES:

3.1 Drafting a Learning Goal

Working in groups of two or three, use the Journal Assignment 3.2. Draft one learning goal, some strategies to meet it, and ideas for monitoring progress toward that goal.

3.2 Discussing a Sample Contract

Discuss the sample contract provided in Form 3.1. In what ways is it clearly designed and well balanced? How would you improve it? Remembering that each placement and each student is unique, identify how this sample could be individually adapted.

3.3 Integrating Resources on Diversity

Think of the populations you will be working with. Identify a group to learn more about. Determine several resources to help you increase your knowledge and skill with this population. Build these resources into your learning contract.

LEARNING CONTRACT
Form 3.1

Student Name: _____

Agency Name: _____

Field Instructor's Name: _____

1. MICRO GOALS

Goal   **Strategies**   **Evaluation**

2. MEZZO GOALS

Goal   **Strategies**   **Evaluation**

3. MACRO GOALS

Goal   **Strategies**   **Evaluation**

_____   _____
Student Signature   Field Instructor Signature

_____   _____
Faculty Liaison Signature   Date

ADDITIONAL READINGS:

Graybill, C.T., & Ruff, E. (1995). Process recording: It's more than you think. *Journal of Social Work Education, 31*(2), 169-181.

Harrison, D.F., Wodarski, J.S., & Thyer, B.S. (Eds.). (1992). Cultural diversity and social work practice. Springfield, IL: Charles C. Thomas.

Kutchins, H. (1991). The fiduciary relationship: The legal basis for social workers' responsibility to clients. *Social Work, 36*(2), 106-113.

Lum, D. (1992). *Social work practice and people of color: A process stage approach.* (2nd ed.). Pacific Grove, CA: Brooks/Cole.

Schwartz, G. (1989). Confidentiality revisited. *Social Work, 34*(3) 223-226.

Wilson, S.J. (1978) *Confidentiality in social work.* New York: Free Press.

Wilson, S.J. (1980). *Recording: Guidelines for social workers.* New York: Free Press.

Stage One

Beginning

STUDENTS REPORT:

Feeling like a stranger, then a guest

Feeling vulnerable and self-conscious

Being enthusiastic about assignments, yet fearful

Feeling anxious about meeting other staff

Feeling overwhelmed

STUDENTS NEED:

- A safe place to share concerns with seminar members and faculty liaison
  Permission to be learners; to understand learning styles
  To build self-awareness of strengths and limitations
  To identify support systems
- To discuss feelings and questions with field instructor
  To be introduced at the agency, to have a place to sit, to leave coat, papers
- Clarification of roles, expectations, and policies
  A written orientation plan
  A plan to focus goals and meet general requirements
  To individualize placement
- To understand how to use supervision in planning and reviewing work
- Skills to start work assignments

- **Indicates a focus of this chapter**

Chapter Four

Beginning the Work

Will I be any good? Will I harm the client?
I can handle intake - it's just like a new customer.
What am I supposed to do here?
What this woman needs is to discipline that kid.
Why would they listen to me?

VIGNETTE

"I'd like for you to talk to this little boy." Amina looked at the intake form. It didn't say much:

Bobby Matthews; age eight, second grade;
Referred by classroom teacher, Pam Jones.
Reasons: Student is often tardy and does not seem to have
        adequate warm clothing. He has few friends and
        appears withdrawn in the classroom. Academic
        performance is very poor.

Amina glanced up at her field instructor. "I wonder if Bobby's depressed. Teachers keep telling me so many of these kids are. It'll probably be hard for him to talk to me. I could even remind him of his mother. Besides, what can I do? Maybe Bobby should see the psychologist instead. Or there's the Friendship Group! I should get on this quickly...tomorrow morning would be best. Will you be here in the morning if I need to know how to refer for testing?"

"Amina," her supervisor said, "Take a deep breath! Now, where should we begin?"

DEVELOPMENTAL FEATURES

Although the beginning stage may vary from a few weeks to a few months, one of the most critical events in this stage is seeing the first "client." Although students are feeling more comfortable as orientation progresses, they are often surprised at how anxious they are when they get their first "real case." Even experienced students indicate that their comfort level is lower when the first real "work" is assigned in their practicum. This work may be a person to interview, the first call on a crisis line, the first presentation in a community education program, the first time to lead a support group discussion, or the first committee meeting for a organizational project.
Whatever the work is, students worry whether they will be any good at it, and fear that they might even harm a client or hurt the organization.

Amina, for example, felt like she'd had a good orientation to the school, was satisfied with both her learning contract and the way her relationship with her supervisor was shaping up. She looked forward to her days at the school, feeling this placement was just perfect for her. Yet her anxiety about meeting Bobby was evident.

Working with your field instructor, however, you can prepare for this new step. We suggest the following:

- Tune in to feelings
- Prepare to explain your role
- Get ready to listen for unspoken messages
- Plan how to review and learn from this specific experience

TUNING IN

Tuning in means taking time in advance to imagine what feelings or reactions you are likely to encounter in an interview, meeting, or situation (Shulman, 1984). It is similar to looking over a map before you take off on a hike: You can get a rough idea of the lay of the land and the obstacles you may encounter. Tuning in can sensitize you to observe more carefully and react more skillfully. However, no map totally prepares you for the realities of a rugged hike, and tuning in is only a tentative beginning skill.

Working with her supervisor, Amina can begin to tune in on many levels. She has already begun to think how Bobby might react to her, but she can imagine his reactions more carefully: How might a child feel being called out of class? Where might he feel most comfortable to talk? Does Bobby likely think of school as a place to get help and have fun or as a place of fear and shame? Will Bobby have any idea what a social worker is?

Tuning in has aspects beyond the micro situation. Amina may also want to tune in to:

- the feelings of the teacher who made the referral;
- the group situation in the classroom when Amina takes Bobby out of the room to talk;
- his family's reactions to this referral; and
- Amina's own feelings as an African American working with a teacher and client who are not.

In tuning in, identify first the major players or factors in the micro, mezzo, and macro aspects of the situation at hand. It may be easiest to begin with one individual, like Bobby, but then to fill in the other people in his world who will also be involved and the issues that may concern them. Thinking about all the levels will help you to take a social work perspective from the very beginning. Larry Shulman (1982) suggests that it is easier to tune in when you can imagine yourself in a situation similar to your client's. It is also helpful to pay attention to your own feelings. Amina is nervous, wanting to "do a good job" and unsure what is expected of her. Who else in this situation may be experiencing similar feelings?

As you tune in, you may identify issues and refer to your human behavior in the social environment texts. Amina could refresh her understanding of what to expect from an eight-year-old boy: Where might he be developmentally? What kinds of peer relationships or group experiences may he be ready for? What would be possible symptoms of childhood depression? What effects can poverty have on children and their families? What can she learn about cross-cultural issues in helping relationships?

Another important aspect of tuning in is to identify value differences that you may encounter. Again, it is important to look at these from a social work perspective. Ask yourself how comfortable you currently are working with this client, family, group of people, or community:

- How well do you understand what they see as their strengths and challenges? How well can you . see the issues involved from their perspective?
- How well do you understand their goals (what they most want) and their methods, options, and barriers to reaching these goals?
- Do you, because of your own values, see their strengths and challenges, goals, options, and barriers differently?
- What do you feel, do, and say about those differences? How might your feelings, language, or actions affect your work together?

Even if you tune in through private reflection, you will benefit from the give and take of tuning in with your field instructor. Doing so will help your field instructor understand how ready you are for the case assignment and how to help you. Field instructors will be able to add to, or clarify, your understanding from their own experiences with similar clients or situations. Of course, there will be surprises! Tuning in only sensitizes you to look and listen more carefully. Do not allow it to blind you to the uniqueness of a particular situation. After the interview is over, your field instructor will be interested to know what happened that you expected, and what surprises you had not predicted.

EXPLAINING YOUR ROLE

If your first job as a social worker is to be sensitive to the feelings and situations of the people you work with, the second job is to understand how you might be of service to them. While people have fairly clear expectations of teachers, realtors, plumbers, and dentists, most people are baffled by social workers. Only if <u>you</u> really understand your role can you explain it well to those you work with. By explaining your role clearly, you provide clients with information so they can choose how and whether they will make use of your services (Shulman, 1982).

Like an orchestra, the roles of all staff in an agency or organization are designed to blend together to respond to an identified mission. The agency is responsible to its community to deliver services in response to that mission under the direction of those who govern the organization. When you can see the whole as well as the parts, you are better able to play in harmony and assure that services are delivered efficiently and effectively. You are also better able to identify gaps or inconsistencies in the quality of services. As you pass through initial agency orientation and begin to represent the agency by delivering services yourself, check periodically to see if you can answer these questions:

- The mission of this agency is...
- The purpose of this unit/service/program is...
- The main focus of a social worker here is...
- The social worker's purpose in this task is...

You may need to refer back to agency material, and to notes from interviews with other staff. Ask these questions - over and over - as you work with your supervisor and other employees. Check out your impressions with your supervisor. Write out your answers and keep them for future reference. You will always need to be prepared to explain your role clearly and simply to those with whom you work.

One reason social work is difficult to explain to the public is because it is an adaptable profession whose role varies widely in different settings. As field seminar members share their understandings of social work in different settings, students will better understand the wide range of functions that social work serves. Perhaps just as importantly, you can together begin to identify the commonalties of the profession in perspectives, skills, knowledge, and values.

PREPARE TO LISTEN FOR UNSPOKEN MESSAGES

Once you have tuned in to the feelings of the client, family, or group and explained your role, you will better be able to listen for the questions or concerns they are reluctant to voice (Shulman, 1984). Listen to some of the conversation between Bobby and Amina in the first meeting:

Bobby: What are you going to do to me?

Amina: I'd like to talk to you and get to know you better.

Bobby: Will my mom be here?

Amina: No, just you and me today.

Bobby: What did I do now?

Amina: Oh Bobby, you're not in trouble! Your teacher asked me to see how you liked school, because she thought you looked sad sometimes. She thought maybe you and I could find ways to make school easier for you. What do you think of that?

It took awhile, but Amina finally understood Bobby's real question: "Am I being punished?" In new situations, especially when we are feeling uncomfortable or scared, we often hide unspoken messages inside cover questions. These unspoken messages are often ones that we think we aren't suppose to ask, or questions we aren't sure we want the answers to. Field instructors may ask students if they like the agency when they really want to ask whether the supervision is working. Students may ask field instructors whether they can take a few days off when they are really wondering how to handle the stress of the work. People ask social workers a variety of "polite" questions to try to determine answers to other questions. What might be the meaning behind these questions social workers are often asked?

Do you see many families like us?
Have you ever been beaten yourself?
Do you live in this neighborhood?
Do you have any other Indian kids you see?
You're only a student?
You seem pretty young. How long have you worked here?

Anticipate that you will get questions like this and think in advance about what they might mean. Try out some responses to them, remembering to check out whether your ideas about the underlying message are on track: "Are you wondering if I'll be able to understand what it's like in this neighborhood?" When you listen for the hidden message, you are better able to avoid feeling defensive and can respond more honestly. You can learn to step out of the expert role and be a human being. "No, you're the first Indian kid I've talked to. I don't really know what it's like for you here. What could you tell me about it?" Human beings respond better to human beings than they do to experts.

You may want to review your practice texts on interviewing before you see a client for the first time, look over information on groups before you facilitate one, or review the duties of a committee chair before the meeting. These would be excellent ways to prepare, not only for the responsibility, but also for meeting with your field instructor beforehand. Usually, your field instructor does not know exactly what you are studying in school. By sharing the knowledge you have from course material, you can get your field instructor's ideas about how best to use it. You have then set the stage to move on together into other material your field instructor thinks may be helpful to you.

REVIEW YOUR WORK

This chapter has focused on anticipating and planning in advance for new responsibilities. While stepping into roles that require you to perform in a new way, remember that you are essentially a student and that the purpose of your work in this placement is to help you learn. As you plan for new assignments, realize that you will not remember everything to ask, the "right" ways to respond, or all the important information you need to know. You will continue to learn by building success, identifying new approaches, and, most importantly, reviewing your work. Chapter Five will examine the role of supervision in this professional learning.

When our work is reviewed, we often feel vulnerable. Talk with your field instructor about how you are feeling and the timing as well as type of feedback you are ready to hear. As the practicum progresses through the stages, students usually are able to seek out and receive more in-depth and specific feedback. We emphasize throughout this book the importance of increasing self-awareness and have just discussed tuning in to the client. Feedback is very important as we work on these skills. It is important to probe into one's own thoughts and feelings, to develop empathy for the client's unspoken thoughts and feelings, and to assess the entire interaction, not just selective parts.

There are many tools to help obtain more specific feedback about your work, including video or audio taping, direct observation, or process recording. Process recordings are a written, verbatim recollection of the interaction between a student and client (individual, family, or group), together with the student's commentary of feelings and thoughts during the interaction, and an assessment of what was happening. Process recordings are very time consuming, yet when used judiciously, can provide feedback that audio or video taping cannot. Students may want to complete a process recording during the first month of work and then one at the end of the practicum, as well as an audio or video tape each quarter.

When you return to your field instructor to discuss work you have already done, be ready to give an honest appraisal of your experience: what went well, what went badly, what else you need to learn. It seems like whenever our work is observed, whether by tape or in person, it is never a "typical" session and often seems not to have gone as well as a session usually does. Acknowledge this with your field instructor and then move on to discuss the feedback. Even if the session was not "typical," you can learn from discussing it. You are responsible, in many ways, for the depth and breadth of your learning by how honestly and openly you evaluate your work. This is not only the hardest part of being a student, but the most important part of being a professional.

In this stage, Beginning the Work, we are no longer dealing with learning in the abstract. The struggle of the student role becomes more tangible when your client refuses to talk, the group member blows up, or the neighborhood representative asks the question you are not prepared to answer. Be ready to continue learning even as time progresses and you gain experience. Your field instructor, and other agency staff, no matter how experienced, will agree that each new client, group, meeting, or presentation can feel like the first time again.

JOURNAL ASSIGNMENTS:

4.1 Reflecting on Highs and Lows

Briefly describe the high point and the low point of your field experiences each week. Identify what you need to talk about further and with whom. Begin to look for patterns of highs and lows.

4.2 Explaining Your Role

Complete the answer to a client's question: "What will you be doing for me?"

4.3 Exploring Value Differences

Thinking of a specific client or group, complete the questions on p. 60 or on p. 63.

SEMINAR ACTIVITIES:

4.1 Presenting Your Work

Students present their work using the outline in Form 4.1. The work may involve an individual client, group, family, community, or project.

4.2 Identifying Social Work Roles

Write on a board one or two social work roles each member has in his or her practicum. Each member states the role in a sentence, but writes only two or three key words on the board. Students discuss the list as a whole to identify both variety and commonalty in social work practice.

4.3 Integrating Coursework and Field

Think of the work you will be doing in your practicum. Bring in one relevant text and one assignment from a class you are taking or have completed. Discuss with your seminar how you will use this information at your practicum. Discuss this information with your field instructor at your next supervisory conference.

WORK PRESENTATION

Form   4.1

STUDENT'S NAME: _____

AGENCY: _____

PLEASE DISGUISE ALL IDENTIFYING INFORMATION

1. Brief description of client system (individual, family, group, community, project, or issue).

2. Goals, strategies, ways to monitor and evaluate (complete Work Goal Chart).

3. Strengths to work with:

4. Barriers to work with:

5. One or two specific questions for seminar's input:

WORK PRESENTATION
GOAL CHART

ONE WORK GOAL FOR EACH LEVEL	A STRATEGY TO MEET THAT GOAL	A WAY TO MONITOR & EVALUATE PROGRESS TOWARD GOAL
MICRO		
MEZZO		
MACRO		

REFERENCE:

Shulman, L. (1982). *The skills of helping individuals and groups* . (2nd ed.). Itasca, IL: F.E. Peacock.

ADDITIONAL READINGS:

Brill, N.L. (1995). *Working with people: The helping process.* (5th ed.). White Plains, NY: Longman.

Freed, A.O. (1988). Interviewing through an interpreter. *Social Work, 33*(4), 315-319.

Perlman, H.H. (1979). *Relationship: The heart of helping people.* Chicago: University of Chicago Press.

Shulman, L. (1992). *The skills of helping individuals and groups.* (3rd ed.). Itasca, IL: F.E. Peacock.

Stage Two

Reality Confrontation

STUDENTS REPORT:

Stress: often get the flu or a cold, become a bit depressed
Becoming disillusioned with agency, field instructor, social work classes
Wondering if social work is a good fit for them
Wondering if social workers can do any good
Sometimes wanting to give up or change placements

STUDENTS NEED:

- To talk with peers, field instructor, and faculty liaison about doubts and fears

  To reflect on how they handle stressful situations; to use stress management skills

  To examine their expectations of themselves

  Permission to make mistakes and take risks

  To identify discomforts with agency, field instructors, social work profession

  Assistance with major problems, crises, and decisions

- To explore feelings about support, authority, independence
- To build a solid supervisory relationship with field instructor
- Effective supervisory conferences
- Skills in giving and receiving feedback

- **Indicates a focus of this chapter**

Chapter Five

Building Skills in Supervision and Feedback

The thrill is gone! What happened?
Do I have to meet with my field instructor regularly?
What is supervision all about?
When can I work more on my own?
How can I tell my field instructor what upsets me?

VIGNETTE

Rosa leaves the following message for her field instructor one Monday about six weeks into her practicum: "Roberto, I won't be in today. I think I'm sick or something. I can't believe it's Monday already. But I did come in that extra day last week like you asked me, to do that project together. I guess something else came up for you. They said you had been pretty busy. Anyway, I'll try to get over this bug. Could we meet sometime later this week? It seems lots has been going on in the last month and we haven't been able to get together much. Sorry to be gone today; I hope nothing important was planned."

Tension had been building for Leslie. She had started her second practicum at the battered women's shelter with reservations about her field instructor, Janelle, who was only twenty-four. Leslie had raised three kids as a single mom, but Janelle kept criticizing her work with the residents. Finally, Leslie could take it no longer and blew up at Janelle.

DEVELOPMENTAL FEATURES

The phrase, "the honeymoon is over" describes the inevitable passage out of the early experiences of feeling anxious, excited, overwhelmed, and self-conscious. What comes next varies greatly between students, but most experience some sort of "crash" when their energy is low, their enthusiasm is dampened, and what used to seem thrilling now becomes routine. Sometimes this second stage, which we call Reality Confrontation, may pass quietly. It may be no more than a lull between feeling like a guest and feeling like a competent team member, but often students become disillusioned, stress builds up, and sadness or illness set in.

Chapter Six will examine more closely the specific aspects of Reality Confrontation: making big mistakes, ethical issues, safety, stress management, harassment, and major decisions. This chapter will examine how, through developing your relationship with your field instructor and using feedback effectively, you might build a source of support and gain skills to handle those difficult issues that may arise.

UNDERSTANDING SUPERVISION

Why Do I Need a Field Instructor?

Building the relationship between you and your field instructor and making good use of your supervisory time together may be the most important ways to insure a good field practicum. Your field instructor is the person primarily responsible:

- for working with you in the agency to monitor your learning;
- for teaching you about social work and, in particular, social work in this agency;
- for supporting you in your learning;
- for pushing and challenging you;
- for evaluating your work and giving you feedback; and

- for assuring that you provide ethical, competent service to clients.

If you have not had a professional supervisor before, you may be uncertain about what is involved this critical relationship. Or, if you have had an unpleasant experience, you may be anxious about this one. No easy recipe exists for creating the "perfect" relationship with your field instructor. Learning styles, past experiences, personality types, the nature of the work and agency, and the stage of development in the practicum all influence the development of this relationship in powerful ways. We suggest, however, four components to explore that may help you to understand what is working, the direction in which you would like the relationship to go, and how to discuss these things with your field instructor:

- Styles of support
- Levels of independence/readiness
- Issues of authority
- Balancing task and process

Styles of Support: Verbal and Emotional Encouragement

What does getting support mean to you? As you reflect on different relationships, you will notice a wide variety in the support you offer and receive; yet, support will be nearly always closely connected with availability. Field instructors vary in how physically available they are - having time to talk - and how emotionally available they are - being able to hear you. The pressures of their own work certainly affect their availability to students. In addition, students' needs vary. Some need to vent about a difficult situation immediately in order to deal with it; others need distance from the event to think about it or write about it before they can accept support.

What do you consider supportive? You may have only considered good news to be supportive. We often learn to feel best when we hear what we want to hear. But encouragement ("the putting in of courage") can mean pushing you to do something you are reluctant to do but which would result in valuable learning for you—learning that you can do this thing, learning why it is important, learning that you aren't ready yet and why. Field instructors and students vary on the balance they prefer between assurance and challenge, and in the timing and conditions under which they are willing to encourage and be encouraged in different ways.

How is a supervisor different from a friend? Can you be "friendly"? How much of your personal life can you share or will you be asked to share? How much support should you expect when your child is sick and you come late for field? Even though professional boundaries are specifically addressed in the NASW Code of Ethics, the line between personal and professional will vary with each person and each relationship. Consulting with your field instructor and others about boundary issues will be important throughout your placement.

Levels of Independence/Readiness

How soon can you act on your own? In what situations are you encouraged to take the initiative? In what cases should you check with your field instructor before you take action, and what do you need to report after you have taken action? In the beginning stages of a practicum, many field instructors want the student to check in more often than they require later on. In the middle stages, some field instructors may want a student to take more initiative and the student holds back. Some field instructors are given more leeway by their own administrators in how much autonomy they can allow their students. Talking about expectations and readiness are important throughout the practicum.

What if you aren't yet ready? For students. taking on some activities will be easier than others. For a new person who is an extrovert, seeking out other members of the team to consult on a case is an easier task than for an introvert; an introverted student may feel ready to work independently sooner. Recognizing and talking about your style is an important part of assessing, planning, and monitoring your learning. Exploring with your field instructor expectations about independence and feelings about readiness will get an important aspect of supervision "on the table."

Issues of Authority

What does authority mean to me? Many factors affect the ideas or values we hold about authority, how we feel it should be used, and by whom. Especially important to explore are cultural factors, gender differences, and differences in age. Many authority issues can arise in field education. You are filling a new role as a student, with new tasks, and new lines of professional accountability in supervision. This can be particularly jarring if you are an older student who has perhaps already filled a responsible position and supervised others. Working in a cross-cultural supervisory relationship brings an additional layer of complexity to your work with a field instructor. Some students find it hard to view young field instructors in a supervisory role; they find it more natural to relate to them as friends, or as their parents. An older field instructor may remind you of an authority figure in your own life.

What power do I have? As in any relationship, agreeing on who is in charge, and of what, is critical. In this case, the field instructor has the authority to assign and evaluate your work. You have the authority to ask that decisions be clearly explained, to voice a differing opinion, and to ask for reconsideration or review of matters that directly affect you. Identify the ways and points at which you can have input and exercise opinions.

How do I respond to power? How the field instructor uses power will affect you, and how you respond to persons in authority will also be critical. Your trust that power will be used fairly should grow as the relationship with your field instructor develops. The development of that trust, however, will depend on previous experiences of both parties. The level of trust will affect your willingness - and that of your field instructor - to take risks in being open and vulnerable. It is important that you and your field instructor examine the tendencies and expectations about control and perfectionism you both carry. It can also be helpful to explore how the use of authority affects the first two components of your relationship: support and independence.

Leslie, for example, resented a younger, less experienced woman's authority over her. She did not respect or trust Janelle's evaluation of her work. Because of this issue with authority, Leslie was willing to accept only positive comments, which she considered to be supportive, and wanted Janelle to leave her alone. Rosa, however, had a different response to authority. In her family, a woman did not question an older man's directions and did not speak up about doing things differently.

Balancing Task and Process

<u>What will we actually do together?</u> Meetings between you and your field instructor involve some combination of task and process. The task discussions include who is the next assigned client, what resources are available, what legislation impacts this agency, what community leaders are the key people to involve, what strategies to use to lobby for your client group, and how to complete a form. The process discussions revolve around how you are feeling about your work, and about the relationship between you and your field instructor. Leslie and Janelle were in this crisis because they had addressed only task issues and had not processed the impact of their own styles and needs on their relationship. Before moving on, they would need to discuss these issues openly to improve their relationship.

<u>How can I improve supervision sessions?</u> The balance between the two dimensions of task and process in supervisory sessions is also influenced by field instructor and student styles and preferences. Some days you may not be ready to reveal your

feelings, or your field instructor may be less able to listen and hear. The two of you will vary in how much task detail you think is important and how to best learn those details. As you become more comfortable in the student role, it will be important to take your share of responsibility for setting the session agenda to better meet your needs. Begin to ask for what you need, whether it is more structure and details about tasks, or more time to process your relationship and your reactions to a certain client or issue.

An effective tool for supervision is to keep a special notebook or file for recording what you need to discuss together with your field instructor and what you have discussed and decided in previous meetings. Remember to record the date of your discussions. This information can assist you in focusing your time together, remembering assignments or agreements, and improving the feedback you provide.

You might want to include:

- work assignments and deadlines;
- modifications to goals or strategies in your learning contract;
- specific information you need;
- issues you'd like to discuss in supervisory conferences;
- day-to-day uncertainties, dilemmas, reactions; and
- your feedback about how supervision is going.

We have not taken a cookie cutter approach by prescribing some unattainable ideal supervisor. These four components always influence how your relationship with your field instructor forms, but good learning occurs in a variety of shapes. Exploring the differences you and your field instructor bring to these components, especially if there are gender, age, or cultural differences between you, will be an ongoing process as you discover new strengths, admit your doubts, set goals, and share successes.

FEEDBACK: A CENTRAL SKILL

In social work, since there are no correct answers to equations or formulas to follow, feedback is essential to our learning and progress. The potential sources of feedback are all around us as we practice: clients, agency staff, neighborhood workers, yourself, and your field instructor.

When we receive information about our work, however, many factors affect our response, including our past experiences with feedback, confidence level, and trust in and respect for the person giving the feedback. Some people, when they receive any positive feedback, blush, discount it, and feel undeserving. Others interpret any negative feedback as punishment, become defensive, and also discount it as undeserved. Feedback will be more effective when "loaded" lables are avoided, when suggestions are offered for possible improvements, and when objective information is shared openly (Ayers, 1995). Basic guidelines for feedback are provided in Table 5.1. The acronym SPIN may help you remember some simple guidelines when asking for feedback, or when asking for it in a different way.

Rosa has left Roberto several subtle messages on his voice mail. Rather than communicate her needs and feelings so indirectly, Rosa needs to provide Roberto clearer feedback. Until she is comfortable giving feedback face to face, she could state her needs in writing. Notice how she uses the SPIN guidelines in the following statements:

- *I need to talk with you about our supervision sessions - would Thursday be convenient for you?*
- *I appreciated your trusting me to complete the project last week, but I was really nervous that you weren't here to double check my work. I'd like to figure out with you some way I could get your feedback on my work before it's finalized.*
- *I really am interested in meeting with you regularly for supervision. I appreciate your ideas and support. I know you are busy, too. What would work well for you?*

SPIN
Table 5.1

GUIDELINES FOR ASKING FOR AND GIVING FEEDBACK

- **S - Specific**
  Ask your field instructor to describe specific behavior that he or she appreciates or wants to suggest changes in. "I would like you to comment on my summary to the group - was it an accurate summary of the group's decision?"

- **P - Positive**
  Ask about behaviors that are working well, changes already made, goals already accomplished, positive suggestions for change. "I think I'm being more assertive with handling those boys' remarks. Have you seen a change for the better?"

- **I - I Messages**
  Ask for feedback using I messages. This helps you to identify your own issues, thoughts, and feelings, and take responsibility for being part of the relationship. "I really need to hear from you about how I am handling my priorities."

- **N - Negotiate**
  Ask for feedback in order to open discussion, realizing that your field instructor may not be ready to discuss the subject yet or in the terms you suggest. Note also that various perceptions are possible and the "truth" may be a combination of both your own impressions and those of your field instructor.

It is important to give and receive feedback regularly and in a timely fashion. Do not rush in when feelings are most volatile and expect to remember how to use these pointers. On the other hand, feedback needs to be given close to the event so that those involved have clearer memories of what happened and negative feelings have not had a chance to build and get in the way. Neither student nor field instructor should put off feedback - positive or negative - until final evaluations. When feedback is regular and timely, we can use it to build trust and make thoughtful changes. It is an important part of an open, honest, and developing relationship.

This chapter discusses two tools available to handle the often difficult second stage of your practicum. A supervisory relationship characterized by openness and willingness to learn increases the trust level between the two of you, building a firmer base when challenges arise, and enhancing learning. Feedback skills can assist you in developing that supervisory relationship, and are also transferable to your work with individuals, groups, and larger systems.

JOURNAL ASSIGNMENTS:

5.1   Thinking about Support

Write a journal entry about how you give support in three different relationships. What do you need in order to feel supported? How do you communicate what type of support you appreciate, is valuable, or helpful?

5.2   Thinking about Authority and Power

Write a journal entry about an experience you have had involving someone else's use of authority and power. What happened? What did you do? Identify how this experience has influenced your current feelings and behaviors around issues of power and authority.

5.3   Reflecting on Seminar Participation

Take time soon after your field seminar meeting to write reflections about your group experience and participation. What did you learn about social work? What was your participation like? What did you learn about yourself? How well is your group working? In what ways would you like to improve your group participation? We suggest repeating this exercise monthly.

SEMINAR ACTIVITIES:

5.1   Role-Playing   Feedback

Using vignettes from the beginning of the chapters or situations you are encountering in field, role play giving, or asking for feedback. Discuss together how to use the SPIN guidelines.

5.2   Discussing   Supervision

Discuss together: What is one thing going well in my relationship with my field instructor and one area that needs improvement? Ask each person to specify one step he or she will take to improve that relationship.

5.3 Discussing Midpoint Evaluation

Discuss with your faculty liaison whether a formal evaluation should be completed midway through your placement. If so, discuss the process and forms required. Refer to Form 9.1 for ideas regarding process and topics for evaluation.

ADDITIONAL READINGS:

Alberti, R.E., & Emmons, M.L. (1995). *Your perfect right* (7th ed.). San Luis Obispo, CA: Impact Publishers.

Ayers, J. (November, 1995). Learning processes in supervision. (Available from Walk-In Counseling Center, 2421 Chicago Avenue, Minneapolis, MN 55404.)

Johnson, D.W. (1990). Increasing your communication skills. Expressing your feelings verbally. In *Reaching out: Interpersonal effectiveness and self-actualization* (4th ed.), (pp. 105-179). Englewood Cliffs, NJ: Prentice Hall.

Johnston, N., Rooney, R., & Reitmeir, M.A. (1991). Sharing power: Student feedback to field supervisors. In D. Schneck, B. Grossman, and U. Glassman (Eds.) *Field education in social work: Controversial issues and trends* (pp. 198-204). Dubuque, IA: Kendall/Hunt.

Barretta-Herman, A. (1993). On the development of a model of supervision for licensed social work practitioners. *The Clinical Supervisor, 11*(2), 55-64.

Kaiser, T.L. (1997). *Supervisory relationships: Exploring the human element.* Pacific Grove, CA: Brooks/Cole.

Stage Two

Reality Confrontation

STUDENTS REPORT:

Stress: often get the flu or a cold, become a bit depressed

Becoming disillusioned with agency, field instructor, social work classes

Wondering if social work is a good fit for them

Wondering if social workers can do any good

Sometimes wanting to give up or change placements

STUDENTS NEED:

- To talk with peers, field instructor, and faculty liaison about doubts and fears
- To reflect on how they handle stressful situations; to use stress management skills
- To examine their expectations of themselves
- Permission to make mistakes and take risks
- To identify discomforts with agency, field instructors, social work profession
- Assistance with major problems, crises, and decisions

  To explore feelings about support, authority, independence

  To build a solid supervisory relationship with field instructor

  Effective supervisory conferences
- Skills in giving and receiving feedback

- **Indicates a focus of this chapter**

Chapter Six

Confronting Difficult Issues

Get me out of this place!
Why am I in social work anyway?
I really don't think my field instructor can help me learn!
I can't talk to my field instructor about this. Who else is there?
I'm having trouble sharing with my seminar group.

VIGNETTES

Ken drags into seminar ten minutes late. He sits slumped in his chair and doesn't look at anyone. When it is his turn to check in, he says, "I think I'm going to leave my placement at Memorial Hospital. Dr. Jones got mad at me for not making discharge plans for a patient, even though the physical therapist said the patient was not strong enough to be alone and home care couldn't start until Monday. And then I called a woman about taking her father home and found out that the man had died the night before but I hadn't checked before I called her. And my field instructor only makes red marks on my patient dictations; she NEVER says anything good about what I do. I'm ready to leave. I'm thinking about trying the preschool program where Mary Alice is; they appreciate what you do and the government isn't shoving people out the door before they are ready to go home! I may even change my major to education. And I've got four papers due, my back is acting up and so is my car."

Everyone is stunned. Ken is usually so upbeat! Mary Alice, sitting next to him, simply smiles and comments: "Everything is fine at my placement!" Pedro mentions that his field instructor is leaving the agency, "but I'm not upset about it. She was really bossy." Blaze admits, "I'm really bummed. I really connected with this eight-year-old kid at the neighborhood center. He came every day and we talked. They moved him to a foster home and he isn't coming back and I didn't get to say good-bye. I felt like crying."

The last person to check in is Jean. She turns to Ruth, the faculty liaison, and asks, "Should I tell them?" Getting a nod, Jean announces, "I have left my agency. They were so homophobic I couldn't learn anything. I felt harassed by their constant comments. Ruth came out and we terminated my practicum. I'm relieved and yet so angry."

DEVELOPMENTAL FEATURES

As we discussed in the last chapter, the honeymoon may be over. For some students, the transition may be a quiet one, and some report never leaving the honeymoon phase. For others, however, the transition comes abruptly and even dramatically; suddenly nothing seems to go right. During this time difficult issues often arise which many students, and sometimes field instructors, have little experience with and feel at a loss to handle. The difficulties can vary tremendously in type and magnitude, but most deal in some way with differences in expectations or feelings of safety. If these issues are not resolved, they can cloud the remainder of this practicum and affect future work. Recognizing these issues and gaining the skills to confront and handle them are the tasks of this stage and the focus of this chapter.

When difficult issues arise, some students resolve them fairly easily and others may find themselves in the middle of a major crisis. The seminar group may find this a trying phase. Often it seems that there is not enough time to deal with each member's feelings and experiences, to problem solve, to follow up, to celebrate—to meet everyone's needs in a balanced way. This is the point where the group may need to confront its own issues and individuals may need to examine their own group behaviors to become more productive members. Just as the difficult issues in the agency provide a chance for individual students to develop new understanding and skills, this stage can allow the seminar group itself to move to a higher level of development.

Usually this stage does not last very long, but it can be intense and stressful. If you recognize and confront issues as they arise, however, you can learn a great variety of skills and move toward feeling more confident in your practice.

WHY CONFRONT DIFFICULT ISSUES?

"Confrontation" has overtones of anger and conflict. Most simply, however, confrontation just means to meet face to face. The examples of issues in Table 6.1 explain why some people might not want to face such difficulties. The examples involve strong feelings or fears, cultural differences, disappointments, or mistakes. We may have strong messages from our growing up years that these types of feelings are inappropriate to discuss, that "nice people" keep these things to themselves. Or perhaps we have experienced blowing up or crying in intense situations. Directly discussing culture, homophobia, racism, age, gender, or sexual matters is almost always a challenge.

Yet it is also obvious how these issues directly affect social work practice and learning in the field setting. Ignoring such matters can result in rising resentment or anxiety. Students may try to avoid the person or situation involved, and miss opportunities to learn or neglect responsibilities. As in any relationship, major issues left undiscussed between a student and field instructor or coworker tend to sit in the corner like large dangerous animals and impede you in discussing all other matters. A student who feels a field instructor has betrayed a confidence or overstepped a boundary will not feel safe using supervision and, ultimately, the work will suffer.

Each of these issues affects how the student functions as a social worker. Jean found it impossible to learn in a hostile atmosphere. She and Ruth directly confronted the field instructor, realized the situation would not change, and terminated the placement. Jean has learned the value of working with the faculty in confronting and resolving this issue. Pedro, on the other hand, has lost an opportunity to understand his supervision needs, his reactions to authority, and maybe even the impact of his culture on his practice. Increasing self-awareness and developing skills in

EXAMPLES OF DIFFICULT ISSUES
Table 6.1

Differences in Expectations

The other student seems to get more responsibilities than I do.

I had hoped to be able to facilitate a group on my own.

My field instructor is very formal; I feel uncomfortable.

*The director was furious that I told the kid myself that her
      weekend pass had been denied.*

I've never worked for an African American before.

*My field instructor was disappointed that I forgot to do it. I feel
      demolished.*

*This agency sounded so good, but they're only concerned with the
      bottom line!*

*I just want to leave! Why do we need to meet with the field
      instructor?*

Nothing about social work is what I expected. I don't think I like it.

Feelings of Safety

My field instructor is telling everyone how I screwed up.

You want me to "explore my feelings" all the time. That's just not me!

*I told my field instructor my husband and I were separating, He said I
      did seem to have trouble relating to men.*

I felt so attached to that child. It tore me up when he was discharged.

*At first I was pleased to meet for supervision over dinner. Now it feels
      odd.*

*I have to do home visits, but there's rats and weird people all over the
      streets!   Will I get shot in some gang war or drug deal?*

John, the other social worker, keeps telling me dirty jokes. I hate it!

dealing with cultural differences, professional accountability, boundaries, strong feelings, and other difficult issues are essential tasks in professional development, beginning in field.

THE IMPORTANCE OF USING CONSULTATION

The situations above are difficult because they involve complex subjects, feelings, perceptions, and interpretations. Most involve power or expectations in relationships between people. The student in each is intensely connected—maybe feeling vulnerable or defensive, having a lot at stake in the outcome of the situation. For just these reasons, situations like these require consultation with someone else to help determine what is going on and what could be done about it. Consultation differs from supervision: In a practice dilemma, the supervisor has authority to choose a specific option for a supervisee, who is then accountable to the supervisor for following this course of action. Consultation involves brainstorming ideas or soliciting advice from those with expertise in a given situation.

Who can provide such consultation? Students sometimes begin with friends or family, who often may lack understanding of field education or social work and may be too close to offer a fresh perspective. Another worker in the agency may also seem like a good choice at first, but please beware! Students who discuss supervisory problems with a field instructor's own coworkers or administrators are setting up a dynamic that often backfires, damaging both supervisory and collegial relationships. This does not mean that you cannot consult coworkers for some types of information. An outreach worker could be valuable to help you feel more safe in home visits; a Mexican American coworker can help you understand a migrant family you are working with. When you consult about a complex issue, in fact, you may be encouraged to interview others in the agency for help with specific, identified needs.

The best choices for consultation are probably within your social work program. Often consultation is one of the primary functions of the field seminar group. Your group understands the experience of field, and its unique demands, and can be a safe and confidential place for you to discuss difficult issues. The Peer Consultation Exercise (Seminar Activity 6.3) might help you focus on what help you would like from your group. Your faculty liaison can also be an excellent consultant. Liaisons may know you well as a learner, may be familiar with your agency or field instructor, and may have a wider perspective on field education and options available to you.

Consultation brings you perspective first of all. Many field students need help, for example, handling mistakes or reprimands. Your seminar group and faculty liaison can help you to sort out what situations you are responsible for and which ones you are not. They can help you determine whether a mistake is minor or major. Ken, in the vignette, will now probably always check on a patient's condition before he calls a family. The family may have been sad or irritated, but this was not a disaster. Consultation can help you pay attention to how you react to making mistakes, or being "called on the carpet." Some students become very defensive and project blame onto others; some feel destroyed if they cannot always be perfect; and some are embarrassed and feel like running—from the agency and even the profession. With consultation, you can identify how to learn from what has happened.

Consultation can help you to identify what steps to take next. Some situations represent a crisis and immediate steps will be recommended strongly. If you have been physically threatened, for example, you may blame yourself and be reluctant to report the incident, but doing so can help the agency better ensure workers' safety in the future (McLaughlin, 1993). Situations that may involve legal issues or mandated reporting may be clarified through consultation. Often situations involving crisis—a client's death, for example, or a neighborhood disaster—deeply affect social workers, both new and experienced. Consultation can help you identify what further processing or counseling you may need to handle these kinds of experiences.

More often, however, difficult situations are chronic rather than acute. This contributes to the difficulty in recognizing them and feeds the—usually futile—wish that they will improve if left alone.

Consultation can help you move beyond a stagnant or hopeless perspective on a chronic, difficult issue. Consultation can provide further useful information. For instance, knowing about third-party payments may help a student understand why the agency is concerned about the bottom line. Sometimes consultation helps to identify information that is missing and ways to gather it. Perhaps the student in the example who was reprimanded by the director needs to learn the specific policies on weekend passes.

Through consultation, also, issues can be carefully analyzed. For example, ethical issues can be discussed using ethical models, such as the one in Table 7.3 in Chapter Seven. Boundary issues are especially complex and often develop subtly over long periods of time. What is the difference between being friendly with clients or coworkers and being unprofessional or even unethical? It is clear that sexual relations with clients is a serious ethical violation, but what about physical roughhousing with the boys in the group home, or hugging the woman whose house just burnt down? Understanding a complex issue can be both easier and more enjoyable in consultation with others.

Finally, consultation helps you to determine the steps to take to resolve difficult issues. Knowing that options exist can reduce your feelings of helplessness, apathy, or anger and move you past being overwhelmed and immobilized. The support of good consultation, whether from an individual or a group, can help you to see that you have a right to address an issue, that you have the skills to do so, and that others care about the outcome of your efforts. The interest of others and their follow-up of your situation can motivate you to take just that first step toward resolving a difficult issue.

SKILLS FOR CONFRONTING DIFFICULT ISSUES

Assertiveness

Social workers need to be assertive to advocate for their clients and speak out on difficult issues. Being assertive about your own needs in a practicum is a good place to develop these skills further. The foundation of assertiveness is the belief that each of us has a right to voice an opinion or a need. This is a skill; we must distinguish assertiveness from aggressiveness and from passivity. Even more complex, we must distinguish assertiveness from manipulation or passive-aggressive behaviors. To qualify as assertive, a message must be respectful and clear. The SPIN guidelines for feedback in Table 5.1 in Chapter Five can also help you be assertive in communicating your needs. Assertiveness does not guarantee, however, that the outcomes will be what you hope for all the time. Through being assertive, you let others know your needs and opinions so that they have the information to act accordingly.

Assertive communication is useful in handling difficult situations that involve differences in perceptions or judgments. For example, a field supervisor may assume you are disinterested in regular supervision if you come unprepared. Rather than being a victim or bad-mouthing the field instructor, you can be assertive by explaining that you would like more guidance in how to prepare and more information about the purpose of supervision. Issues involving differences in culture, gender, or age may also benefit from assertive communication. If these issues are not brought <u>onto</u> the table, they will continue to influence relationships <u>under</u> the table.

Expectations play a major role in our adjustment to and satisfaction with social work and our practicum experience. While it is important to be optimistic and positive, we also need to assess and monitor whether the expectations we have are reasonable. For example, if you are disappointed that you were left out of an activity or missed saying good-bye to a client, you can communicate clearly what your hopes are. Agencies can be busy places and decisions must often be made quickly. In addition, since you are the "new kid on the block," the agency will not be accustomed to factoring in your needs as decisions are made. Assertively communicating about expectations is an important step in discovering if modifications need to be made.

Negotiation

Because differences can be expected whenever people work together, whether in a multidiscplinary team, a community group, or with one other person, negotiating skills are useful to develop. It is important to remember that the <u>process</u> of negotiating is as important as the outcome. The atmosphere, feelings, and communication styles in the negotiation process can set a positive tone, enhance personal insight, and increase the likelihood that future issues will be more readily negotiated. A few key concepts to remember in negotiating:

• Be prepared. Spend some time thinking about the issue, the goal of your work, the facts, and some alternatives; take time to be focused.
• Clearly identify the differences as you begin to discuss the issue. Where do expectations diverge? Try to get all the facts on the table and describe the conflict or difference as objectively and nonjudgmentally as possible.
• Be respectful. Attack the problem and not the person.
• Listen carefully. Only in this way can new information surface, options be explored fully, and solutions be generated that best meet the needs of those involved.

Recontracting is a specific type of negotiation that is often useful in handling difficult field issues. Recontracting may follow an open discussion between you and your field instructor, for example, about your expectations for doing groups, or a perception that you may lack cross-cultural exposure. When you want a change, let your field instructor know in advance that you would like to discuss recontracting. Set a time and place where you will not be interrupted and bring copies of your current learning contract. If you are running into barriers in recontracting, you and your field instructor may want to meet together with your faculty liaison.

Stress Management

Learning to manage stress is an important skill for handling difficult issues. While we think of it as something to avoid, sometimes stress can be positive, energizing, or motivating. We may feel stress, for example, when taking positive steps toward handling other difficult issues by being assertive or negotiating.

Stress management is an ongoing process; there are times when we manage better than others. When papers are due, the car will not start, and the doctor is upset with us, our reactions are different than if only one of these situations happens at a time. Most of us have ways to manage stressful situations. Some work harder, others become immobilized, some eat, some smoke or drink, others exercise or play. Some need to be alone, others need to talk. Being aware of our positive and negative ways of coping, and then building the positive into our schedule, is an important lifelong process. Remember that support systems help us cope. Refer back to Journal Assignment 1.2 to review your support systems. Have you been tapping into them? Are there others you could add to the list? Sometimes our reaction to stressful situations signals a need for more professional help.

In the vignette, Ken's back probably acts up more when he is under stress. If his back did not hurt and his car worked, he might be more creative in handling the angry doctor and more forgiving of himself for calling the family before checking on the patient. Ken might add a goal to his learning contract:

Goal:
To more effectively manage stress

Strategies:

1. Begin a stress journal
2. Read two books on stress management within two weeks
3. Implement two strategies from the reading in my daily life
4. Exercise back every night before bed; chart progress
5. Take every Sunday afternoon off to play with my family
6. Talk to two social workers about job stress

Evaluation
1. Review stress journal with my wife each week
2. Discuss new strategies and their effectiveness with my field instructor

3. Review progress chart on back exercises

4. Compare 1st week stress journal entries with last entry.

These three skills - assertiveness, negotiation, and stress management - can help you implement ideas you gain from consultation about difficult issues. Recognize that these skills are the same ones you use in your social work practice to help clients, groups, committees, or communities confront the difficult issues they, too, experience.

To end this chapter we will address four specific difficult issues that field students sometimes encounter: sexual harassment, changing field instructors, changing agencies, and leaving the social work program. Even though you may not encounter these issues, read the rest of the chapter to understand what other students may be experiencing and how you can be supportive to them.

SEXUAL HARASSMENT

A significant number of undergraduate and graduate field students experience sexual harassment. Although the victim is usually female, males are also harassed (Shank, 1986). The perpetrator, male or female, is often in a position of authority, such as a faculty member, field instructor, or administrator, but may also be another student or another worker in the agency. Sexual harassment may include a number of behaviors involving unwelcomed sexual advances or requests. It may be verbal, physical, or psychological in nature; it may involve only one incident, repeated incidents, or even a generally hostile or offensive work environment. Examples include:

- promise of a good evaluation for sexual favors;
- constant efforts to change a professional relationship into a personal one;
- persistent and offensive sexual jokes, cartoons, or comments;
- jokes or comments demeaning to a particular gender; and
- unwanted physical contact such as patting, pinching, or touching.

Sexual harassment in field is a serious concern because it interferes with a student's learning. When you feel intimidated or unsafe, you will not be able to perform well, or work well with the person who is harassing you. Sexual harassment used by others as a term or condition of future employment or field placement can result in unfair rewards or threats.

If you are believe you are being sexually harassed, remember that this behavior is unethical and you have a right to report it. Do not allow the perpetrator's intimidation to stand in the way, even if you are unsure of what to do or believe you can endure the situation. Even if you are involved in a consenting romantic or sexual relationship with a faculty person or field instructor, the power differential is so significant that mutual consent is usually not possible. Such relationships are usually also considered sexual harassment. Generally, those who harass you will have harassed others and your actions may prevent someone else from being hurt in the future. We suggest taking these steps:

- <u>Tell the harasser to stop</u>. Be specific. If they do not stop, keep a record of their actions and yours. Keep in mind your personal safety.
- <u>Get support.</u> Talk with someone who will listen to you and support you. Consult your program's policies on sexual harassment and report the problem to the appropriate person as soon as possible.
- <u>Get counseling</u> if you need it. This may be a crisis that requires immediate intervention and perhaps longer term counseling.

CHANGING FIELD INSTRUCTORS

During the year, a student's field instructor may change, which may be welcome or unwelcome. If the relationship is a positive one and the field instructor leaves the agency or can no longer continue as a field instructor, the student may be devastated. Often another social worker is available and a new field instructor is named. Communication among the school, student, and old and new field instructors is critical. Information about the school's requirements, the student's work to date, and future goals need to be shared. While starting over may be frustrating, the important work needed to create a relationship with the new field instructor will be familiar.

If the relationship has not been a good one and the change is made because of unresolvable conflict, the issues are a bit different. The faculty liaison may be helpful in negotiating the change to a new field instructor and in identifying the changes that need to be made in order for this relationship to be successful. Specifically, the problems need to be identified, and strategies should be discussed and agreed on by the new field instructor and student. It is important to resolve negative feelings, when possible, if the people are to continue to work in the same agency. At a minimum, each party must agree not to slander the other. For example, Pedro, in the vignette, must not gossip about his field instructor's bossiness. It may feel good to tell everyone who will listen what the other person did wrong, but this is unprofessional behavior that also reflects badly on you.

CHANGING AGENCIES

Students normally remain in the same agency for the duration of the practicum. When difficulties arise, explore alternatives in order to avoid unnecessary disruptions:

- Discuss the situation with your field instructor. Usually differences can be resolved.
- Discuss the situation with your faculty liaison. Perhaps a meeting with the three of you can result in important changes.

However, circumstances do arise which require a change: the agency may close, the only qualified field instructor may leave, there may not be sufficient clients, or the differences between the learning styles and personalities are too great to accommodate the learning of the student. As in Jean's case, an agency may be unethical. Whatever the reason, following a careful process can make the change less difficult. Consult your faculty liaison about any policy your school may have. If no policy exists, the following steps can be a guideline:

- Agree with the field instructor on the process for termination with clients and agency staff.
- Ask your field instructor for a summary of your work and issues that led to changing placements.
- Write you own summary statement of your work and issues that led to changing placements.
- Discuss with the faculty liaison: the process for selecting another placement, what information from a previous placement will be shared, what goals need to be addressed in the new placement, and the total hours required in the new placement.

It is important to keep the termination as positive and respectful as possible. You are constantly building your professional reputation.

LEAVING THE SOCIAL WORK PROGRAM

Making the decision about whether social work is the "right fit" is an important and often difficult step in a college career. While some students may voluntarily choose to leave social work, others may be asked to leave the program. It is as important to learn if social work is not a good fit for you as it is to learn that you will be a dynamite professional. The decision to leave social work can be a positive one when you have considered your strengths and alternatives and have carefully discussed your choices and options with people who know you and can help you. The decision should not be made in haste or as a reaction to a mistake or to stress. In those cases, taking a leave or short break is recommended, so that a decision can be made more thoughtfully.

If you do decide to leave social work, remember to inform important people of your decision. These would include your academic advisor, the director of the program, your faculty liaison, and field instructor. They can help you identify others that may need to be informed. Closure is important in all areas of life; giving attention to a strong ending will help you move on more easily.

Students may be asked to leave a social work program based on their failure to meet established standards, inability to function professionally, inability to acquire the necessary skills within the time frame of the program, or violation of professional standards or unethical behavior. Students who are asked to leave have the right to appeal this decision; follow your institution's grievance or appeals procedure. For students involved in this situation, receiving appropriate support is critical.

When a student whom you know is asked to leave the program, it is difficult for you, too. Because of confidentiality, you may not know all the information, and the student and faculty liaison are not able to share it with you. Taking sides is tempting, but unless you have all the information this can be hurtful. Our best advice is to be as respectful of the process as you can, be as involved and supportive as appropriate, and decide what lessons can be learned.

Confronting reality is a "growth opportunity." Usually students move beyond this stage with greater confidence and competence. The challenges inherent in identifying issues and dealing with them can be painful and require courage, honesty, support, and understanding in everyone. Individually, you may need to summon the courage to be more honest with yourself and others. Seminar members can play an important part in this struggle; maybe modifications need to be made in your group so you can master this stage together. Your field instructor and faculty liaison have experienced many struggles and are valuable resources. In your journey to become a competent professional, confronting difficult issues may be one of the most significant steps.

JOURNAL ASSIGNMENTS:

6.1 Beginning a Stress Journal

- List your signs of stress (body reactions, thoughts and feelings, behaviors)
- List what triggers your stress
- Create your stress relief list: things that you do to relieve stress. Include a variety: physical (diet, exercise), mental and spiritual (meditation, "thought-stopping"), and environmental (activities with friends, volunteer work, hobbies).

6.2 Reflecting on Highs and Lows

Briefly describe the high point and the low point of your field experiences each week. Identify what you need to talk about further and with whom. Begin to look for patterns of highs and lows.

6.3 Evaluating Your Group Participation

Evaluate your <u>own</u> participation in the field seminar group with Form 6.1.

Evaluating Your Group Participation
Form 6.1

Mark each item below whether you demonstrate the role:
A = All of the time; S = Some of the time; N = Never.

Productive Roles: I...	Counterproductive Roles: I...
_____ Initiate discussion	_____ Act with aggressiveness or hostility
_____ Give useful information	_____ Distract group from focus
_____ Ask for ideas or information	_____ Act with defensiveness
_____ Give positive reactions or opinions	_____ Act superior or all-knowing
_____ Ask for reactions or opinions	_____ Withdraw
_____ Give constructive feedback	_____ Am absent
_____ Ask for clarification	_____ Do not actively participate
_____ Comment on the group's movement or lack of it	_____ Am dominating
_____ Encourage others	_____ Come late or leave early
_____ Arrive promptly	_____ Carry on side conversations
_____ Remain attentive	_____ Exclude some members
_____ Appropriately disclose struggles	

SEMINAR ACTIVITIES:

6.1 Whining Together

Have a whining session followed by a brainstorming session on stress relievers:

- Set a timer for three minutes. Taking turns, each person names one stressor as quickly as possible; keep taking turns until the timer rings.
- Then set the timer for six minutes. Have a brain storming session on stress relievers: one person writes all ideas on the board that people have found helpful in relieving stress. At the end of six minutes, each person writes two ideas they will try, and add them to their stress journal relief list.
- Finish this exercise by placing your hands on the shoulders of the person next to you (you may want to stand and form a circle here) and giving a shoulder massage.

6.2 Role Playing Difficult Situations

Role play a difficult situation brought up by one of your group members. Let the person choose the role they want, have another person play the other part. One group member keeps track of whether they are using the SPIN model; the rest give positive feedback as well as different ideas to try.

6.3 Using Peer Consultation

Complete Part 1 of Form 6.2 to prepare for seminar group consultation on an issue you need help addressing. Complete Part 2 afterward.

6.4 Evaluating Group

Complete the following questions individually, ranking each item from 1 (poor) to 5 (excellent). Then discuss together what changes to make in your group to better meet members' needs.

```
┌──────────────────────────────────────────────────────────┐
│                    Group   Evaluation                      │
│                                                            │
│ _____   Our  group  sessions  encourage  identification  │
│          with  professional                                │
│          social  work  values  and  ethics.               │
│ _____   Our  group  members  provide  mutual  support    │
│          for  each  other.                                 │
│ _____   Our  group  members  provide  valuable  and      │
│          honest  feedback  in  a                           │
│          way  that  helps  my  learning.                   │
│                                                            │
└──────────────────────────────────────────────────────────┘
```

REFERENCES:

Kuechler, C.F. (1994, April). *The Consultation Circle: A framework for peer consultation in field seminar.* Paper presented at the 1994 Biennial Midwest Social Work Education Conference, St. Paul, Minnesota.

McLaughlin, F.X. (1993). *Violence against social workers: When the helper is hurt.* Unpublished masters thesis, College of St. Catherine/University of St. Thomas, St. Paul, Minnesota.

Shank, B.W., & Johnston, N. (1986, March). *Sexual harassment: An issue for classroom and field educators.* Paper presented at the Annual Program Meeting of the Council on Social Work Education, March 1986, Miami, Florida.

ADDITIONAL READINGS:

Davis, M., Eshelman, E.R., & McKay, M. (1988). *The relaxation and stress workbook.* Oakland, CA: New Harbinger Publications.

Fisher, R., & Ury, W. (1991). *Getting to yes.* New York: Penguin Books.

Jacobs, C. (1991). Violations of the supervisory relationship: An ethical and educational blind spot. *Social Work, 36*(2),130-135.

Johnson, D.W. (1990). Resolving interpersonal conflicts, Confrontation and negotiation, Anger, stress and managing feelings, and Barriers to interpersonal effectiveness. In *Reaching out: Interpersonal effectiveness and self-actualization* (4th ed.), (pp. 215-324). Englewood Cliffs, NJ: Prentice Hall.

Kuechler, C.F. (1998).   The Consultation Circle: A model for team consultation. In A. Daly (Ed.), *Workplace diversity: Issues and perspectives.* Washington, D.C.: NASW Press.

Lerner, H.G. (1986). *The dance of anger.* New York: Longman.

Maypole, D.E., (1986). Sexual harassment of social workers at work: Injustice within? *Social Work 31*(1) 29-34.

Pollack, D. (1997). *Social work and the courts: A casebook.* New York: Garland.

Reamer, F. (1994). *Social work malpractice and liability: Strategies for prevention.* New York: Columbia.

Richard, R., & Rodway, M.R. (1992). The peer consultation group: A problem-solving perspective. *The Clinical Supervisor, 10*(1) 83-100.

PEER CONSULTATION REQUEST
Form 6.2

Name: _____   **Date:** _____

Prepare Part I before seminar. Complete Part II to turn in before the next seminar.

Part I

1. Briefly describe the issue, incident, case, or problem for which you are requesting the group's assistance. Provide adequate information, but omit any identifying data.

2. Formulate a focused question for the group.

Part II

1. Summarize the feedback or suggestions the group provided.

2. Follow-up (complete before the next seminar and turn in). Describe what actions you've taken and what outcomes have resulted since the last group.

3. Integrate. What specific social work knowledge, values, and/or skills are useful for understanding and responding to your issue?

Source: Adapted with permission from Kuechler, C.F. (1994).

Stage Three

Relative Mastery

STUDENTS REPORT:

Feeling more confident and competent
Learning to leave worries at the agency
Continued anxiety about new assignments, working with clients
Reaching a compromise between reality and expectations
Willingness to discuss value dilemmas

STUDENTS NEED:

- To take more initiative in own learning, become more self-directed
- To explore new challenges
- To continue building relationship with field instructor
- To evaluate feedback
- To evaluate own practice
- To build on strengths and interests
- To identify what learning they still need
  To find ways to contribute to the agency

- **Indicates a focus of this chapter**

Chapter Seven

Shaping a Professional Self

How do I know if I'm doing any good?
That feedback just wasn't fair!
I love what I'm doing! I want to learn more!
What if I don't like that client?
This seems like an ethical issue....

VIGNETTES

Tamicka is in a bind. She is working with a mother, Shanna, who just got some money from her children's father. He had never paid child support before, but last week won $1000 in the lottery and gave Shanna half. If Tamicka reports this gift, the county will reduce Shanna's check, but if Shanna can just pay for her car repair, she can finish school and take a job that's been offered! Shanna's car conked out last week, and without it she can't take the job. Tamicka has been trying to find another way to fix the car, but there is nothing available. Should Tamicka pretend she never heard about the money? Her field instructor is very strict about punishing clients who lie, but wouldn't Shanna's getting a job be worth it?

Lisa knocked on her field instructor's office door. "Sam, do you have a minute?" Sam motioned Lisa to sit down and suddenly she began to cry. Sam handed her the box of tissues. "What's up?" he asked softly. "It's this family I saw today. I don't think I can work with them! They're having lots of conflicts but can't discuss them at all. I don't know what clicked inside but something made me ask about health issues. They seemed reluctant, but eventually shared that the dad has a heart condition and they're all afraid to upset him. But then I just froze up. My father died of a heart attack. Shouldn't I be over it by now? I really want to do more work with families, but what if I can't handle my own stuff?"

109

Jasmine wasn't sure what to say to her field instructor about her meeting yesterday with Josey. Josey had shared that her pastor had urged her to return to her husband, that this was her duty. Josey had asked Jasmine if she read the Bible, and did she agree with the pastor? Jasmine had offered some other ideas, and Josey had asked Jasmine to pray with her to help her make up her mind about going home. Was this social work?!

Boris can't decide what to do. The receptionist at the community center is a former client who lives in the neighborhood. Boris has been encouraging the Nguyen family to come in for counseling, but they refuse because they are sure the receptionist talks about clients' secrets in the community. Boris has mentioned this to his field instructor, but has been assured records are confidential. Boris has seen Ty, the receptionist, looking at files, but doesn't want to cause trouble.

Hli is working with refugees from Somalia. Perhaps because her family came to the United States from Laos, she is very aware of the issues facing these families and of the violence in the world. She wants to join the group that is lobbying for a change in the laws but wonders how that will affect her internship. Is she too close to the situation to be taken seriously?

DEVELOPMENTAL FEATURES

At this point in their practicum, most students begin to report a feeling that things are coming together. Comfort levels are higher, relationships are more established, some routine can be counted on. And for many, this stage is the longest and most satisfying portion of placement.

Several ingredients combine to bring about this "in the swing" feeling. Thorough orientation and thoughtful contracting laid a foundation early. The time devoted to developing a good supervisory relationship paid off when issues, misunderstandings, and challenges arose. To the degree that the student and field instructor were able to discuss and work through issues as they were identified, the student is better able to move past any feelings of disappointment into a readiness to learn <u>from</u> the realities of this practicum, not just <u>in spite of</u> them. Each issue identified and resolved, each success and strength celebrated, each challenge or mistake acknowledged, has built the student's capacity to integrate self-awareness, classroom learning, and an understanding of the agency and people it serves.

During this stage, students report consciously thinking of themselves as a professional, rather than an impostor. As this professional self develops you will find it increasingly easy to identify your strengths, understand your growing competence, and recognize and nurture your style. It also becomes less threatening to identify areas for continued growth. Though new assignments will always bring anxiety, this stage of field is characterized by much less stress and a willingness to try new responsibilities that test out just what this new "tool" that is your professional self can do! Most students are ready to move toward being more <u>aware</u>, more <u>active,</u> and more <u>analytical.</u>

MOVING TOWARD A MORE AWARE PRACTICE

The social worker must attend to his or her development as a <u>whole</u> person. Different kinds of work challenges, personal crises, involvement in therapy, volunteer experience, arts and travel, conferences, wide and varied reading, and discussion or support groups can all impact professionals' growing understanding of themselves. With experience, social workers learn more and more about <u>how</u> to increase their self-awareness. We began discussing self-awareness in Chapter One. (You may want to review your personal strength inventory or information on your learning style preference.) In this chapter we continue discussing self-awareness as it relates to personal issues, style, and meaning and spirituality.

Personal Issues That Affect Practice

Lisa, in the vignette, was able to use her own experience to assess the new family, but also became aware that her father's death affected her ability to work with this family. Her story illustrates that growing self-awareness highlights both a worker's strengths <u>and</u>

limitations. Attention to personal issues is a serious ethical concern: What might have happened if Lisa had ignored her discomfort? How should the family be informed if Lisa doesn't continue with them? What does Lisa still need to discuss with her supervisor? How much about this issue is relevant: Lisa's conflicts with her father? Her grieving process? Her heavy responsibilities for her mother? As her supervisor helps Lisa explore this personal issue, how will he and she avoid crossing a boundary into therapy?

Lisa was attuned to how she felt with this family. Social workers need to pay attention to transference (the feelings and associations others have of you,) and counter transference issues (your associations and feelings of those you work with), even when their work is not "therapy." How we feel about those we work with, and their reactions to us, affect outcomes deeply. Review practice and human behavior course material to understand both transference, and countertransference issues. Supervision is necessary to help us explore how these issues factor into our assessments and the way these issues affect work with clients.

While we usually become troubled by strong feelings of disliking a client, we often do not pay sufficient attention to our strong positive feelings toward a client. Yet we must remain aware of how attraction to a client might affect our professional judgment. If we become, essentially, a friend to a client, can we still fill the role as their social worker? Of course, any sexual involvement with a client is a serious violation of the NASW Code of Ethics.

Relationships become quite complicated, especially in smaller communities, for example within a neighborhood like Boris's, in an ethnic community, or in a rural area. Through your work you may know things about your son's new friend, or find yourself in a professional relationship with someone you know from church. Workers in such situations report feeling they must closely monitor their behavior outside the workplace and work hours. What—if anything—will they say to a client over the cabbages at the grocery store or at a bar ordering drinks? Many tell clients at intake that, to protect confidentiality, they will wait for the client to acknowledge them in public. Because dual relationships are potentially a violation of the NASW Code of Ethics, consultation with colleagues is essential.

Differences of Style

Students often enjoy working with a number of people in their placement because they can observe different styles, trying each on for size and constructing or refining a personal approach. With experience, we have each realized that, within professional and ethical guidelines, many styles can be "right." As you become more aware of and comfortable with your own style, you can begin to construct a flexible practice repertoire—understanding when a particular aspect of that style is more likely to be effective, and what unique gifts you have to offer.

Clues to your style can be found in how you prefer to start or end a work day, in the way your desk looks, in the tasks you enjoy, in the responsibilities you avoid. The choices in Table 7.1 explore some style factors; they are not meant to be exhaustive, or to represent clear polar opposites. They may, however, help you to identify and begin to discuss what is meant by style and how it affects your work.

Familiarity with your style can also assist you in knowing what groups or tasks present a challenge to you. If you enjoy a "fly by the seat of your pants" approach, what skills might you need to develop in order to chair a committee? If you depend on structure to a great degree, how will you handle crises? What settings might require a worker comfortable with confrontation? When are humor and self-disclosure helpful? Reflecting on questions like these will help you identify areas for continued professional growth.

DEVELOPING A PERSONAL STYLE
Table   7.1

Formality, reserve	Informality, openness
Large, busy work settings	Small, casual work settings
Use humor, gentle teasing	Serious, careful not to offend
Maintain privacy, keep "me" out of the picture	Self-disclosure of feelings or experiences
Stress areas of agreement	Comfortable with confrontation
Speak own opinion easily; move to act quickly	Need much time to reflect, hear others, weigh issues
Enjoy following	Enjoy leading
Provide direction, motivations, opinions, interpretations	Avoid making decisions for others; careful not to influence
Prefer process, big picture, creative brainstorming	Prefer tasks, detail, implementation
Prefer variety in responsibility	Prefer to focus on fewer tasks
Prefer working independently	Prefer collaboration
Need structure, planning timelines	Adapt well to surprises, see what happens, comfortable with last minute changes
Learn best from discussion, workshops	Learn best from reading, independent study

Meaning and Spirituality

Social workers often find that professional identity has deep and even spiritual meaning. The values on which social work rests are powerful. We have often been attracted to the field because of harmony between those values and our own personal, political, and sometimes religious values. The work involves us in relationships with people coming to grips with the deepest aspects of human experience: family, violence, health, unemployment, poverty, oppression, disasters, infertility, personal change and growth, matters of life and death. We see others at their most vulnerable and most resilient.

This adds another facet to social workers' professional growth and identity. Everything from experiences with clients to events in the political arena challenge our purpose, motivations, and directions for practice. Like Jasmine and Hli in the vignettes, we are often confronted with helping individuals, groups, and communities make sense of their experiences on many levels. Besides providing another window to diversity, spirituality is being explored by some social workers as a potential assessment and intervention tool. It presents, however, complex dilemmas regarding boundary roles and self-determination. As your field experience advances and deepens, you may find that you are interested in exploring the implications of spirituality for social work practice. Many of us find, also, that we must identify multiple ways to nurture ourselves through the demands of practice: physically, emotionally, mentally, and spiritually.

MOVING TOWARD A MORE ACTIVE PRACTICE

The experience of field education is unique, for all the reasons discussed in Chapter One. Learning how to learn in this way is particularly challenging for students who are unused to "hands-on" education, unfamiliar with professional roles or supervision, and new to the skills of social work. However, as your practicum progresses, so do expectations that you will not only become more comfortable, but also take more responsibility for improving your learning. Since these skills remain central to professional development, we have called them "Active Practice Skills." Table 7.2 describes some characteristics of active practice.

The micro-level skills involve integration of practice experiences with theoretical classroom learning, your self-awareness of a variety of issues, and your willingness to continue to challenge yourself to learn more. The mezzo level deals with your interpersonal relationships, especially teamwork and feedback skills. Although we have discussed feedback, even using the SPIN method we may get a response that is unexpected or punitive. Handling these situations is difficult for even seasoned professionals, and a more active practitioner uses additional skills. The macro-level skills relate to your involvement in the agency and community and the issues that confront them. Addressing these larger issues is a value of the social work profession.

You may use this list to ask for feedback from your field instructor about your progress as an active learner and practitioner. In Appendix F you will find a checklist to evaluate your practice in terms of the social work code of ethics. We also recommend that you review the evaluation forms your program uses for field students as a gauge of your progress, and to continue to make your learning contract an active part of your planning, supervision, and evaluation.

MARKERS OF ACTIVE PRACTICE
Table 7.2

MICRO

Identify learning needs and increase knowledge
Identify impact of values, feelings, personal issues, and needs
Be intentional about professional use of self
Ground practice in theory
Practice skills of self-care
Cultivate courage to confront challenges
Build confidence through recognizing strengths and successes
Develop effective personal style

MEZZO

Communicate honestly and assertively
Seek supervision
Demonstrate appropriate autonomy and accountability
Engage in teamwork and collaboration
Foster respectful relationships among diverse colleagues and clients
Develop system of support and consultation
Apply agency policies thoughtfully
Improve agencies' responsiveness and effectiveness
Utilize a variety of tools to evaluate practice

MACRO

Be informed about current social issues, needs, changes
Participate in the political process
Pursue social and organizational change
Act to eliminate oppression and injustice
Build connections with and among communities
Broaden understanding of the human condition

MOVING TOWARD A MORE ANALYTICAL PRACTICE

As we increase in self-awareness and become more active practitioners, we find that we are both more aware of the complexities of practice and more competent and willing to struggle with those complexities. Three facets of this more analytical practice are explored below: ethical dilemmas, practice evaluation, and incorporating theory in practice.

Handling Ethical Dilemmas

No matter how long we have been practicing social work or in what setting, we are inevitably faced with ethical issues. We make choices daily in our professional and personal lives without much thought or awareness of the reasons behind our decisions, or the decision-making process itself. Other ethical dilemmas, however, make us uncomfortable and we agonize over them, aware that the issues are critical and overwhelmed by their complexities. When you encounter ethical issues in field, it is essential to seek consultation (NASW Code of Ethics 2.05), but discussing the dimensions of the dilemma is critical in deciding the most ethical course of action.

There are many excellent texts on ethics, and you, no doubt, have studied about ethics in a specific course or in all of your classes. It is helpful to use a model to make thoughtful decisions. A model is meant to be adapted; the important thing is to use it and practice with it so that, rather than making a snap, uninformed decision, you can be thoughtful and deliberate. While many models are available, (see Additional Readings at the end of the chapter), we offer a seven-step guide for ethical decision making in Table 7.3. To clarify how to use it, we will walk through the vignette of Boris and the Ngyuen family. We also refer to the 1996 NASW Code of Ethics when considering professional principles and standards. Information about other Codes of Ethics is included in Appendix F.

Seven Step Model of Ethical Decision Making
Table 7.3

Step 1: Gather relevant facts and information.

-What else do you need to know?
-Do you have the facts and have them right?

Step 2: Identify ethical issues, relevant values and principles, and dilemmas.

-Are there nonethical problems that complicate the situation?
-What is the primary dilemma?

Step 3: Generate alternative courses of action and likely consequences.

-What are all the possible courses of action? (Include doing nothing)
-What are the consequences of each? (good/bad; short/long term)

Step 4: Assess alternatives and consequences in light of relevant values and principles.

-Which values, principles, or standards guide your ethical reflection?
-Is one more important than the others?

Step 5: Assess your motives in light of relevant values and principles.

-What life experiences and/or faith stances might be influencing your ethical judgment?
-Whose interests are being served?

Step 6: Choose an alternative and justify your choice.

-What ethical argument/framework can you give to justify your choice?

Step 7: Evaluate the choice at a later time.

-What, if anything, would you have done differently, and why?

Source: Adapted with permission from Hamel, 1996.

Using the model, we will highlight some of the deliberations Boris might have as he consults others and works through his dilemma with the receptionist and the Nguyen family.

Step 1: Gather relevant facts and information.

> What else do you need to know?
> Do you have the facts and have them right?

Boris needs to find out what the receptionist's job duties are—does Ty have a right to look in the files? Does Ty know about, and have to abide by, confidentiality? Boris knows that the receptionist does talk about cases outside of work because Ty came up to Boris at a soccer game and was talking loudly about one of the clients. It is also important to know that the agency has a grant to employ qualified residents of the neighborhood. What else does Boris need to know?

Step 2: Identify ethical issues, relevant values and principles, and dilemmas.

> Are there nonethical problems that complicate the situation?
> What is the primary dilemma?

The primary issue seems to be one of confidentiality— who has access to the records and the nature of confidentiality in the agency. There are also issues involving boundaries and employment of neighbors. The potential dilemma is a conflict between responsibility to the neighborhood community and confidentiality to clients. What about Boris's responsibility to the agency? to clients? to future clients? to colleagues?

Step 3: Generate alternative courses of action and likely consequences.

> What are all the possible courses of action? (Include doing nothing)
> What are the consequences of each? (good/bad; short/long term)

1. If Boris does nothing, it is possible that the clients will not be served and the family will fall apart, other clients will refuse service, and rumors will be started in the neighborhood by the receptionist.

2. If he talks with the agency director, the receptionist may get fired or the agency could change its employment policy so that no former clients/ neighborhood people can be employed; they would lose the grant, however.

3. He could talk with the field instructor and the team and discuss the importance of confidentiality. The agency could review who has access to client files and make appropriate changes.

4. Perhaps he could give an inservice to all employees. With information about the purpose of the policy and consequences, employees may be more conscientious about following the policy.

5. What are other alternatives and consequences?

Step 4: Assess alternatives and consequences in light of relevant values and principles.

> Which values, principles, or standards guide your ethical reflection?
> Is one more important than the others?

The relevant standards are: Client confidentiality (NASW Code of Ethics 1.07, 2.02, 3.04); Commitment to employers (NASW Code of Ethics 3.09); Ethical responsibility to broader society (NASW Code of Ethics 6.01, 6.04) because the receptionist is a member of a disadvantaged group. Social workers' responsibilities to clients is a primary standard; responsibilities to colleagues, the agency, and the broader society are also important. Which of these takes precedence in this case? Why?

Step 5: Assess your motives in light of relevant values and principles.

> What life experiences and/or faith stances might be influencing your
>   ethical judgment?
> Whose interests are being served?

Boris is aware that he has a hidden issue; the receptionist used to date his sister and abused her. He knows he needs to use care and not be revengeful. He doesn't want the agency to lose the grant money, either, because he hopes to be hired there after he graduates. He is aware of his personal issues and is trying to think of the professional values, too. If you were involved in this case, what life experiences or faith stances would influence you?

Step 6: Choose an alternative and justify your choice.

> What ethical argument/framework can you give to justify your choice?

Boris chooses to offer to conduct an inservice for all employees about confidentiality. He and his field instructor recommend that the agency change access to client files and discuss with each client how confidentiality is maintained in this agency. In order to assure trust in the community, a task force is invited to work with the agency about confidentiality issues. He chooses this action because, to him, client confidentiality is the most important ethical principle involved in this case. Would you choose a different course of action? Why?

Step 7: Evaluate the choice at a later time.

> What, if anything, would you have done differently, and why?

Boris realizes that he could have mentioned to his field instructor his previous association with the receptionist at the beginning of the placement. Although it may not have changed anything, he would have felt more honest about the issues. At the soccer game, he could have told Ty that it is not appropriate

to talk about clients outside the agency. What would
you have done differently?

This case is relatively uncomplicated. Working through the process,
however, prevents Boris from creating a climate of mistrust or even
being responsible for the loss of Ty's job. Striving for high quality
ethical decisions is an ongoing, evolving process. The challenge is to
take the most ethical action you can and continue to develop the
awareness and ability to examine ethical dilemmas. Consulting with
others is an imperative part of the process.

Evaluating Your Practice

Social workers continually ask themselves whether their work
is accomplishing the goals they and others have. The NASW Code of
Ethics holds us accountable to our clients, communities, and
colleagues for effective work (NASW Code of Ethics 1.04, 4.01,5.02).
From the very beginning of the practicum, you were encouraged to
think about outcomes by devising ways to evaluate your progress
toward meeting the field goals in your learning contract.

As you move toward analyzing your practice, review research
course material to see how to apply options for practice evaluation at
your field placement. Find out how colleagues there evaluate the
success or impact of their own work and programs. Often agencies
report service outcomes to funding sources or accreditation bodies.
In addition to practice evaluation, some agencies are involved in
research projects and perhaps your program requires you to
complete research at your placement. If so, you can learn first-hand
how practitioners contribute to the body of professional knowledge,
and how ethical issues of informed consent and confidentiality in
research are handled.

The NASW Code of Ethics (4.01) holds each social worker
responsible for informed and effective practice. Analytical
professionals seek out colleagues with information and the latest
techniques. They read professional journals and publications to stay
abreast of new developments and issues. They review textbooks for
theories and methods that might make more sense at this point in

practice than they did in the classroom! Continuing education requirements for state licenses provide standards for social workers to maintain learning after graduation. As you move toward a more aware, active, and analytical practice, you will also gain knowledge and expertise to contribute to the profession.

JOURNAL ASSIGNMENTS:

7.1 Exploring Personal History

Identify a situation you have had in your practicum in which your own personal history affected your work. Think about how it affected your work.

7.2 Exploring Personal Style

List four words that characterize your style. Reflect on how each characteristic can be both a strength and a limitation.

7.3 Exploring Personal Meaning

Find an image or an object that symbolizes for you the meaning of your chosen vocation of social work. Attach it or describe it in your journal. Reflect on what it represents to you.

7.4 Reviewing Professional Behavior

Review the professional behavior checklist given in Form 7.1. What are areas of strength for you? What do you want to continue to work on?

SEMINAR ACTIVITIES:

7.1 Discussing Personal Styles

Talk with seminar members about your developing personal styles. Add to the list in Table 7.1 by thinking of someone in your agency as well as yourself. Discuss how your style affects your work.

7.2 Using the Seven Step Ethical Model

Practice using the seven-step model: Work through the first vignette of Tamicka's dilemma. Pay particular attention to steps 2, 4, and 5 as you discuss values that guide the decision you might make if you were Tamicka.

7.3 Using Consultation

Seminar members present a current dilemma. Work through the steps of the model. Offer insights and information and identify personal issues that may be involved.

7.4 Applying Research Articles

To stimulate thoughts about evaluating practice, bring an article from a professional journal that includes research about a practice issue. Share the articles and discuss how the research might affect practice at your agency.

7.5 Discussing Practice Evaluation

Make a short presentation about how practice is evaluated at your agency.

7.6 Discussing the Human Condition

Each student chooses a novel, play, poem, film, or other artwork, and discusses with the seminar members how this work informs social work practice.

PROFESSIONAL BEHAVIOR CHECKLIST
Form 7.1

Note to Students: Please rate your abilities in the following areas on a scale of 1 to 4. A rating of "1" indicates you feel you have a major problem with this issue. A rating of "4" would indicate that you feel you never have any difficulty with this issue.

A. Self-Awareness of Personal Issues.

_____1. I disclose personal issues to clients only when the client will benefit from the self-disclosure.

_____2. I share personal issues with the field instructor when they are relevant to work with a client or to my functioning in the fieldwork placement.

_____3. I am aware of and deal with anger and other emotions appropriately.

_____4. I deal with stress and frustration in productive ways.

_____5. I seek outside support and/or counseling when personal issues are creating discomfort or affecting my work with clients.

_____6. I demonstrate awareness and sensitivity regarding cultural, ethnic, and lifestyle differences.

_____7. I am assertive without being aggressive.

B. Self-Awareness of Professional Issues.

_____1. I practice the highest level of confidentiality in dealings with clients and agencies.

_____2. I am accountable to my field instructor for work performed.

_____3. I am reliable in managing time at the agency and discuss absences with my field instructor ahead of time if at all possible.

_____4. I demonstrate appropriate collegial relationships.

_____5. I am responsible for my own learning and seek feedback from my field instructor.

_____6. If my learning contract needs change, I renegotiate it with my field instructor.

_____7. If I have a concern about an agency, field instructor, or colleague, I share the concern with the field instructor first.

_____8. My relationships with clients are professional in nature, rather than on a friendship or romantic level.

Student Signature _____

Field Instructor _____

Source: Berger, Thornton, and Cochrane, 1993

REFERENCES:

Berger, B., Thornton, S., & Cochrane, S. (1993, February). *Communicating a standard of professional behavior: A model for graduate and undergraduate field education.* Paper presented at the Council on Social Work Education 39th Annual Program Meeting, New York, NY.

Hamel, Ron. Seven Step Ethical Model available from Ron Hamel, Ph.D. Director, Clinical Ethics, Lutheran General Hospital, 1775 Dempster Street, Park Ridge IL, 60068.

National Association of Social Workers. (1996). *Code of ethics.* Washington, DC: Author.

ADDITIONAL READINGS:

Corey, G., Corey, M., and Callanan, P. (1988). *Issues and ethics in the helping professions.* Pacific Grove, CA: Brooks/Cole.

Frankl, V.E. (1963). *Man's search for meaning.* New York: Washington Square.

Gambrill, E., & Pruger, R. (Eds.). (1997). *Controversial issues in social work ethics, values and obligations.* Boston: Allyn & Bacon.

Hepworth, D.H. (1993). Managing manipulative behaviors in the helping relationship. *Social Work, 38*(6), 674-682.

Lowenberg, F., & Dolgoff, R., (1996). *Ethical decisions for social work practice* (5th ed.). Itaska, IL: F.E. Peacock.

May, L., & Sharratt, S.H. (Eds.). (1994). *Applied ethics: A multicultural approach.* Englewood Cliffs, NJ: Prentice-Hall.

Reamer, F. (1990). *Ethical dilemmas in social service* (2nd ed.). New York: Columbia University Press.

Rhodes. M.L. (1991). *Ethical dilemmas in social work practice.* Milwaukee, WI: Family Service America.

Sermabeikian, P. (1994). Our clients, ourselves: The spiritual perspective and social work practice. *Social Work, 39* (2), 178-182.

Uehara, E.S. et al. (1996). Toward a values-based approach to multicultural social work research. *Social Work, 41*(6), 613-621.

Westerfeldt, A., & Dietz, T.J. (1997). *Planning and conducting agency-based research: A workbook for social work students in field placements.* New York: Longman.

Stage   Three

Relative   Mastery

STUDENTS REPORT:

Feeling more confident and competent

Learning to leave worries at the agency

Continued anxiety about new assignments, working with clients

Reaching a compromise between reality and expectations

Willingness to discuss value dilemmas

STUDENTS NEED:

To take more initiative in own learning, become more self-directed

- To explore new challenges
- To continue building relationship with field instructor

To evaluate feedback

To evaluate own practice

- To build on strengths and interests
- To identify what learning they still need
- To find ways to contribute to the agency

- **Indicates   a   focus   of   this   chapter**

Chapter Eight

Taking Risks

Is this agency doing all it can?
That seems unethical to me!
But these are social workers—how can they be so racist?
I know it's not right, but what can I do about it?

VIGNETTE

Kim's practicum is in a family service agency that provides a variety of counseling and educational programs. She has helped with the three parenting groups: an "enrichment day out" that takes preschoolers and their mothers to cultural events on Tuesday afternoons, a Friday morning support group for parents whose children have learning disabilities, and a Monday night court-mandated group for parents who have been reported for child abuse. Kim is noticing that the parents attending the Tuesday and Friday groups are at least middle class, while the court group seems low income and much more diverse ethnically. Agency social workers complain that the court group's attendance is sporadic, members are late, and discussion is minimal. Kim is wondering if the group accomplishes anything. She has some ideas, but has been assured they wouldn't work because of the "challenging population." Kim wants to ask the executive director if the agency is really committed to providing quality services for the whole community, but she is reluctant to bother him.

DEVELOPMENTAL FEATURES

The last chapter described how students in this stage of field find themselves ready to move into a more aware, more active, and more analytical practice. In this chapter we will explore further how increased competence and confidence guide appropriate risk taking in social work practice.

As students feel more comfortable in their role as social workers, they become more confident in taking risks. Rather than viewing practice dilemmas or agency quirks as discouraging roadblocks, many students develop a strong interest in taking on these challenges. They begin to navigate the disparities between the real and the ideal in both the agency and the profession as a whole. This wider perspective can assist them to set priorities, negotiate appropriate compromises, and strategize for needed change in the agency, community, or profession.

This chapter will explore how students can understand the issues of differences and political dynamics in the agency, and how they can use models and skills for effective and ethical risk taking in professional practice.

WORKPLACE DIFFERENCES

Social work practice requires skills to work with differences. "Start where the client is" suggests that we must first be willing to recognize different perspectives, empathize with different feelings, understand different values, and work with others to reach goals they determine for themselves. Differences are basic in working with strengths, and the NASW Code of Ethics (see Appendix F) discusses respecting differences in several ways. Social workers, agencies, and communities, however, have developed in a sociopolitical context that variously ignores, fears, and hates those that differ from the dominant culture. Social workers must realize that oppression impacts all levels of practice, from individual development to dynamics in relationships and groups, to the distribution of power and resources in social institutions.

Most of our chapter vignettes have involved issues of differences. The students have confronted situations made more challenging because of their ethnic backgrounds, their sexual orientation, their age, their learning styles, and their personalities. What are all the reasons Kim could be reluctant to talk with the executive director? Could Kim feel intimidated by his administrative position and his plush office or because he is an older gay white man with a Ph.D.? Is she influenced by other staff, who complain that he is arrogant and murmur that the agency should have a social worker as director? Or is she just unsure whether it is the most appropriate way to handle her concerns?

As students become more familiar with agency people, policies, and practices, they discover how the agency is dealing with differences and can see the impact of those differences on work relationships and services. Terry L. Cross (1990) developed a model that helps both individuals and agencies assess how well they work with differences (see Table 8.1). The model describes a continuum that moves from destructive practices and attitudes, beyond "blindness" to differences, beyond the complacency of tokenism, toward a level of cultural competence.

Kim, from the vignette, might talk with her field instructor to learn more about the services the agency has offered for diverse families, and together they might be able to locate the agency's cultural competence on the continuum. Do the workers' attitudes toward the diverse populations seem dehumanizing? Have they been involved in destructive recommendations to remove children on the basis of race? If the agency does not fit the category of Cultural Destructiveness, perhaps it falls more under Cultural Incapacity. Unintentionally, it might be directing resources disproportionately to white, middle-class parents. Workers may have little information about working with diverse cultures and may have lower expectations and stereotypes of them. Everything from the attitudes of the reception staff to the magazines and art in the waiting room may give subtle messages that this agency's focus does not include persons of color.

Kim feels that she has just moved beyond the middle point of Cultural Blindness. Always feeling that color should not matter, she has assumed that good helping techniques and good services would equally meet everyone's needs. She has focused more on the "deprivation" she saw in other cultures than on learning about the strengths differences offer. At this point, though, she sees herself

CULTURAL COMPETENCE CONTINUUM: AGENCIES AND PROFESSIONALS
Table 8.1

CULTURAL DESTRUCTIVENESS	CULTURAL INCAPACITY	CULTURAL BLINDNESS	CULTURAL PRE-COMPETENCE	BASIC CULTURAL COMPETENCE	ADVANCED CULTURAL COMPETENCE
(is intentionally destructive)	(is not intentionally destructive but lacks capacity to help people of color)	(expresses a philosophy of being unbiased)			
* practices cultural genocide (e.g., boarding schools for Native Americans)	* takes paternal posture toward "lesser" races	* believes that color or culture make no difference; we're all the same	* realizes its weaknesses in serving minorities and attempts to make specific improvements	* has acceptance and respect for differences	* holds culture in high esteem
* dehumanizes or subhumanizing clients of color	* disproportionately applies resources	* believes helping approaches used by dominant culture are universally acceptable and universally applicable	* tries experiments; hires minority staff, explores how to reach clients, trains staff on cultural sensitivity, recruits minorities for their boards and advisory committees	* engages in continuing self-assessment regarding culture	* adds to knowledge base by doing research, developing new approaches based on culture, publishing results of demonstration projects
* denies clients access to their natural helpers or healers	* discriminates based on whether clients "know their place" and believes in the supremacy of dominant culture helpers	* thinks all people should be served with equal effectiveness	* has commitment to civil rights	* makes adaptations to service models in order to meet client needs	* hires staff who are specialists in culturally competent practice
* removes children from their families on the basis of race	* may support segregation as a desirable policy	* ignores cultural strengths, encourages assimilation, and blames clients for their problems	* may feel a false sense of accomplishment that prevents further movement	* works to hire unbiased workers	* advocates for cultural competence throughout the system and improved relations between cultures throughout society
* risks client's well-being in social or medical experiments without their knowledge or consent	* enforces racist policies and maintains stereotypes	* follows cultural deprivation model (problems are the result of inadequate cultural resources)	* may engage in tokenism	* seeks advice and consultation from minority community	
	* promotes ignorance and unrealistic fears of people of color	* practices institutionalized racism			
	* maintains discriminatory hiring practices	* sets ethnocentric eligibility for services			
	* gives subtle "not welcome" messages				
	* has lower expectations of minority clients				

Source: Adapted with permission from Terry L. Cross, MSW, Director
          National Indian Child Welfare Association
          Portland, OR

moving into Cultural Pre-Competence, understanding that she (and maybe this agency) is weak in serving diverse families and wants to improve. Perhaps for Kim a good move would be to identify persons and agencies that exemplify cultural competence, who use the expertise of persons of color to develop responsive multicultural programs. She might offer to collect information or resources for her practicum agency.

Social workers are called to operate in that far end of the continuum where differences are valued and sought out to enhance our understanding and services. Each of us bears responsibility to help our agencies deal openly with how differences affect our work relationships, our policies and procedures, our projects and services, and our use of resources.

WORKPLACE DYNAMICS

An agency or organization is a decision-making structure. Even when the individuals who wrote the agency's original mission and policies are long gone, procedures have been put into place to monitor, interpret, and amend those policies. The administration must make difficult decisions to respond to changing program and budgetary requirements. These procedures and decisions require some sort of organizational structure. Many social service agencies are structured along bureaucratic lines, a model that evolved to formalize decision-making processes and eliminate unfair or arbitrary personal influences in administration. Other organizations are implementing structures that de-emphasize hierarchy and focus on democratic decision making. In some agencies, social work services are the sole or primary focus and social workers find themselves and their work at the center of decision making. However, in other organizations, like schools or hospitals, social work is an adjunct to the "main business." Decision making must take into account the needs and perspectives of many professionals in these guest settings.

As a field student, you have an opportunity to experience agency decision making in a real-world setting, while referring to material in policy courses to help analyze what you see. Gathering information comes naturally in a student role, but it will continue to form the basis of understanding—and changing—the agencies in which you will be employed. However "clean cut" official policies and procedures appear, decisions <u>are</u> personal and workers have an appropriate stake in the way decisions such as these are made.

- <u>Autonomy and accountability in work:</u> Who decides what social workers do? Who evaluates how well we do it? What do we expect of each other?

- <u>Distribution of resources:</u> How will social work be supported and rewarded? What resources will we have: other staff, space, equipment, time?

- <u>Appreciation of professional input:</u> Is social work valued? Can I influence the services or programs I'm involved with? How do we divide "turf" among different professions' perspectives and expertise?

- <u>Efficacy and efficiency of decision-making structures:</u> Do social workers have representation or input? Will my perspective be heard and responded to in a timely manner? Are decisions ethical?

- <u>Consistency and flexibility in applying policies and standards:</u> Is everyone following standards? When are exceptions made? If someone challenges a decision, will it be reviewed by a fair grievance process?

To better understand your agency, ask your field instructor to discuss how the organization makes decisions. You may want to begin by referring back to your agency presentation in Chapter Two. The information you gathered then about the agency's goals, governance, funding, and structure may be more meaningful to you now that you are familiar with the programs. Ask your field instructor to help you to understand other pressures on the agency. Perhaps external licensing, regulatory, or insurance bodies influence the autonomy or responsibilities different workers may have. A shift in funding sources may mean that certain services have priority and others are in jeopardy. Shifts in leadership bring new priorities and energy, but also a period of uncertainty and fear. Your field instructor can describe general trends and pressures in this agency to help you gain knowledge to use both here and in your future work.

When we understand agency administration we usually begin to appreciate its complexities and challenges. Agency missions and goals are often easier to state than to measure and achieve. Programs that sound good on paper may have tremendous barriers to overcome. Flow charts and organizational charts cannot do justice in describing the challenges real people face working together in complex and difficult situations. Yet, despite the challenges, each social worker is responsible for ethical practice involving colleagues, clients, and communities.

WORKPLACE SKILLS

Being responsible for ethical practice means social workers must develop an array of skills. Basic everyday skills such as tolerance and respect form a foundation for the more advanced skills demanded as conflicts emerge and feelings run high.

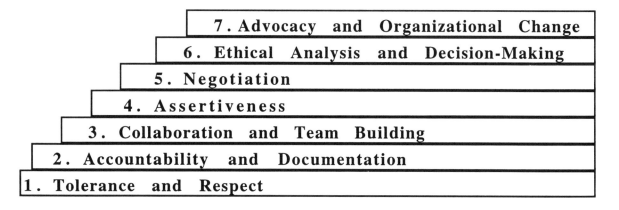

7. Advocacy and Organizational Change
6. Ethical Analysis and Decision-Making
5. Negotiation
4. Assertiveness
3. Collaboration and Team Building
2. Accountability and Documentation
1. Tolerance and Respect

Tolerance and Respect

The more we understand, accept, and work with our own style, the more awareness, patience, and respect we develop for others' differences. Without this base, all other skills will falter. Students are vulnerable in agencies: They often struggle to become part of an agency, and sometimes they are easy audiences for disgruntled employees. It is important to distinguish between information and gossip, and between support and manipulation. This is tricky, even for seasoned workers. Suggestions to help clarify what is going on include keeping an open mind, making efforts to talk with several people and not just one, and consulting with your field instructor and field seminar group. Often just discussing your questions helps to clarify what is happening. When you are asked or expected to take sides or keep secrets, be sure to talk with your faculty liaison or field instructor. Professionals often need to consult about setting respectful boundaries with co workers.

Accountability and Documentation

Workers rely on each other to do what they say they will do and to inform others by documenting their work. When colleagues know that you can substantiate your work, retrieve important information, and leave behind records that are useful for others, your credibility increases. In the case of emergencies, absences, or charges of unethical treatment, documentation becomes especially vital. Though recordkeeping sounds like a petty micro task, it not only forms the basis for good relationships on the mezzo level, but also provides the necessary information to examine agency services and support needed changes.

Collaboration and Team Building

Beyond respect and tolerance, learning to work effectively with colleagues is critical to social work practice. Cooperative tasks maximize the different perspectives and skills of workers, enrich options, and improve outcomes. In some settings, interdisciplinary team work is the mainstay of service delivery. For many, out-of-agency collaborations strengthen the community and make better use of scarce resources. Collaboration with other workers also helps them to get to know and appreciate your skills, and builds a network you can use for support and feedback.

Assertiveness

While most of us understand the difference between passivity, assertiveness, and aggressiveness, a practicum often presents a special challenge. Students may feel more reticent in field since they may be "on the margin" of the work group, have less knowledge or experience in this agency, and are hoping for good evaluations and references. Use feedback skills such as SPIN (see Table 5.1 in Chapter 5) to develop your voice in the agency work. Ask for feedback to determine how you are perceived when you take risks to speak up. A good supervisory relationship is central, also, to developing and monitoring assertiveness.

Negotiation

Negotiation skills will look very familiar to social workers, resembling the problem-solving model and being based on the values of good communication and respect. Refer to Chapter Six for further discussion on the negotiation process. Discussing disagreements will be much more satisfactory with a win-win approach.

Ethical Analysis and Decision Making

Refer to Chapter Seven for a plan to help you navigate turbulent ethical waters. Discussing ethical issues has unique risks for students. In the student role, you may lack some pertinent information, and you may be taken less seriously. Because of the shorter duration of your placement, you may have a different perspective than agency workers who may have seen slow but steady progress on a particular issue. In addition, students often feel vulnerable because they are in need of good evaluations and references from the field instructor and agency. Would Kim be as eager to discuss her agency's cultural competence if she had just recently been asked to interview for a job there following graduation?

Advocacy and Organizational Change

Central social work roles include advocating for the needs of those we serve, respecting individual rights, and working for enhanced quality of life for all. Effective advocacy relies on careful gathering of information, documenting that information, and understanding the mission of the agency or program. Only then is it possible to point out inconsistencies between that mission and actual policies, programs, or procedures.

When you identify an issue, begin discussions first with your field instructor or faculty liaison. Throughout practice, you should always engage a support network and colleagues within the agency as you engage in advocacy and change efforts. A "Lone Ranger" approach can leave you isolated and scapegoated. If you decide with your field instructor or faculty liaison to take action, you will likely begin with the person most closely connected to the incident or issue. Students are sometimes tempted to take a complaint directly to supervisors, administrators, or boards, being reluctant to deal directly with those involved. However, circumventing a thoughtful step-by-step process of organizational change only <u>increases</u> the chances that the change effort will fail and that unnecessary damage will result along the way. For example, by not going to the person directly involved, facts or essential information may be missed and the action taken may be inappropriate. Or, by not consulting someone, your interpretation may be incorrect and could result in hurt feelings, a damaged reputation, or punitive action. Be familiar with and follow the chain of command when working to change an organization. When advocating for a client or for review of a decision, adhere to established grievance or due process procedures.

Rarely do students encounter situations that require them to expose agency practices for public examination. Whistle blowing is a last resort after all internal routes have been exhausted. It is reserved for situations of the gravest concern and requires extremely careful analysis. You should begin with consulting a member of your faculty about any serious concerns in your agency.

As you gain understanding of yourself, of the agency, and of the profession, you will grow in the skills and readiness to take risks to confront difficult situations. Whether those situations involve eliminating discrimination in the workplace, improving the quality of services to the public, or challenging oppressive policies and institutions, social work values and ethics form the basis for personal, interpersonal, and organizational change.

JOURNAL ASSIGNMENTS:

8.1 Measuring Personal Cultural Competence
Locate yourself on the Cultural Competence Continuum in Table 8.1. Tell a story about yourself that describes why you locate yourself at this point. Set one goal to move further along the continuum in respect to one type of difference.

8.2 Improving Workplace Relationships
If you have difficulties relating to a person in your agency setting, use your journal to describe your feelings. What would you like for the relationship to be like? What is one step you can take to move the relationship in that direction?

8.3 Analyzing Agency Policy
Refer back to your agency presentation in Chapter Two. Reflect on how your understanding of your agency has grown since orientation. Identify an area of agency policy, programing, or procedure that you would like to clarify, analyze, and perhaps impact. Develop a plan to gather information on this issue.

SEMINAR ACTIVITIES:

8.1 Measuring Agency Cultural Competence
Identify a diverse population that your agency serves. Make a presentation to your seminar, discussing who this population is, and

analyzing the response of your agency on the Cultural Competence Continuum in Table 8.1.

8.2 Consulting about Workplace Relationships

Using your Journal Assignment 8.2, present a succinct description of the difficulties you experience with someone at your agency. Remember to respect privacy. Ask your group to brainstorm ways you can respond to this dilemma using the skills outlined in this chapter. Report to the seminar at a later date on the outcome.

8.3 Analyzing Agency Challenges

Refer to the questions for discussion with your field instructor on page 138. Prepare a presentation to your seminar based on your understanding of the pressures and challenges faced by your agency and how those might be impacting decision making, resource allocation, and employees.

8.4 Integrating Coursework and Field

Identify specific information in a social policy textbook that helps you better understand a specific agency's pressures or challenges (Activity 8.3) or helps you decide how to begin to impact them (Activity 8.5).

8.5 Impacting Agencies

Using your Journal Assignment 8.3, share with your seminar group the issue or policy you have identified and the information you have gathered. Ask your group to brainstorm a first step you can take to impact this situation. Report back later on the results of that first step.

8.6 Using the Internet

Choose one of the following options:
- Send an e-mail letter to your legislator about a bill or proposal or issue of interest
- Follow a bill in your state legislature on the Internet

- Bring in five internet addresses that have been professionally useful and share them with other members.

REFERENCE:

Cross, Bazron, Issacs, and Dennis (1989). Towards a culturally competent system of care. Cross, Georgetown University, Child Development Center.

Cross, T.L. (1990). Toward cultural competence: Equipping trainers to train. National Indian Child Welfare Association, Portland, Oregon.

ADDITIONAL READINGS:

Bobo, K., Kendall, J., & Max, S. (1991) *Organizing for social change: A manual for activities in the 1990's.* Washington, DC: Seven Locks Press.

Covey, S.R. (1990). *The 7 habits of highly effective people.* New York: Simon & Schuster.

Gutierrez, L., Alvarez, A.R., Nemon, H., & Lewis, E. (1996). Multicultural community organizing: A strategy for change. *Social Work, 41*(5), 501-508.

Leigh, J.W. (1998). *Communicating for cultural competence.* Boston: Allyn & Bacon.

Rivard, J.D., Madrigal. C., & Millan, A. (1997). *Quick guide to the internet for social workers.* Boston: Allyn & Bacon.

Sue, D.W., & Sue, D. (1990). *Counseling the culturally different* (2nd ed.). New York: Wiley.

Weil, M.O. (1996). Community building: Building community practice. *Social Work, 41*(5), 481-499.

Stage Four

Closure

STUDENTS REPORT:

Feeling ambivalent about ending: sad, detached, relieved, withdrawn

Graduating students report:

> reappearance of self-doubt

> being distracted by new demands - relocating, job search, license exam

First year students report:

> looking forward with confidence to the next practicum

> having clearer expectations for the next practicum

> being concerned about meeting higher expectations for the next practicum

STUDENTS NEED:

- To reflect on past experiences with endings; identify patterns
- To share feelings with seminar members and field instructor
- To start the closure process early
- To develop an ending plan
- To reflect on their growth and learning
- To use learning to develop new goals and future plans

- **Indicates a focus of this chapter**

Chapter Nine

Ending and Looking Ahead

How can I just leave all these people?
Can I volunteer here?
2 days, 4 hours, 16 minutes and counting
When will I see you again?
But I never got to run a group...

VIGNETTE

Doug slipped out the back door at 4:00 PM. He had finished his placement that day. No one had said good-bye. No one had even noticed that he was leaving. His final conference with his field instructor and faculty liaison had been last week and had been OK. The whole year had been just OK. But he wondered if anyone would miss him, if he had done any good at all. He felt lousy. He wondered if he would be any good at his new job.

Uma was glad to walk out the door on her last day. She had to plan her graduation party (her parents were coming for that), take her license exam, write those final two papers, and try to fit in job interviews. She was glad she had started to wind down at field a month ago. No way would she have had the energy for all those good-byes this week.

Reuben wasn't ready to leave. He loved these kids, the people at the agency, and the community. He didn't have a summer job yet, and had told his field instructor that he would stay on and volunteer. He was really good with the kids, and they had learned how to handle the neighborhood bullies. But he wanted to be around for them this summer.

Jeanette was graduating, too. She had had a challenging, exhilarating experience and was hoping to have a job within the agency. Her field instructor had provided an excellent reference and now the director of the department called, asking her to send a resume. She had begun talking about closure with clients several months ago and the staff was planning a luncheon. She was really sad to be leaving, but was ready to move on.

DEVELOPMENTAL FEATURES

As students prepare to end their practicum, they may be exhilarated at what they have accomplished, proud of new skills and insights, disappointed in gaps, or frustrated that the year was not more challenging or satisfying. At the same time they reflect on the practicum and evaluate their growth and learning, they also need to look ahead, build on strengths, make new goals, and plan for further growth.

Students experience a range of emotions during the last weeks of their placement. Feelings range from sad to relieved, very emotional to detached. Many other events are happening in their lives at the end of the school year and it is a relief to have the time once spent in field available for other things. Graduating students are often anxious about finding a job and question their ability to practice. After a particularly difficult job interview, they might think they have learned absolutely nothing! On the other hand, students finishing their first practicum are often confident about their skills and are excited to move into their next practicum.

The way students face endings is affected by both their previous experiences with closure and the relationships they have developed through the practicum. Some, like Doug, avoid closure. Others, like Reuben, may also avoid closure when they have had a positive field experience and do not want to leave; they may volunteer to stay on or keep stopping by for coffee. Planning for a positive ending is a process that starts months before the actual last day. This chapter will discuss that termination process.

HANDLING ENDINGS

Ambivalence, avoidance, denial, grief, anger, joy. People experience a range of emotions when leaving a relationship, a place, a job, or an internship. Many people have not had an opportunity to plan a successful ending; they have experienced only pain. Paying attention to your own patterns of closure will be important as you plan the ending of this practicum experience. Our own issues with endings very directly affect our endings with others. If you begin talking with your field instructor early about your own feelings and thoughts about endings, you will be better prepared for handling issues your clients, groups, or neighborhood committees raise. The journal and seminar activities at the end of this chapter help you reflect on your experiences.

Because endings reawaken feelings of other losses, clients may often surprise a worker with their behavior when told the worker is leaving. Clients may become hostile, their behavior may regress, or they may avoid you or stop coming to appointments. Groups may seem apathetic and stop working. These reactions frustrate, confuse, and anger social workers. It is important to anticipate and plan for endings with clients who often have not had positive closure. If you need additional resources when you and your field instructor plan your termination with clients, refer to your practice texts or to the suggested readings at the end of the chapter.

Fuzzy endings create problems. Plan to end on a clear note with the agency staff, field instructor, and clients. If you will be staying on as a new employee, it is important to end the role as student and clarify what will be the same and what will be different about relationships, tasks, and expectations in your new position. This is also true if you plan to stay on as a volunteer. However, look carefully at your reasons for staying on. Are you staying because you cannot bear to leave, because saying good-bye is difficult, or because you have nothing better to do? Hanging on may sour a good experience; avoidance of saying good-bye is not a reason to stay. Take this opportunity to learn the value of clear, positive endings.

Finishing with a negative attitude about the practicum often means there are unresolved issues that will resurface in the future. Whether the disappointments have been with unmet goals, problems, or relationships, it is important to discuss them, work on what can be resolved, and plan to learn from these disappointments. Growth can be more powerful when it is the result of struggle and hard work. Your faculty liaison and your field instructor will be valuable resources as you decide how to address and resolve disappointments, frame future growth goals, and create a professional development plan. Because negatives can overwhelm the positive, reflecting on and discussing positive aspects of the practicum experience are essential in the work of termination.

Our research has shown that it is common for self-doubt to reappear, particularly among graduating students, near the end of the field placement. When faced with finding a job and taking the license exam, students become anxious and think they know nothing, or at least not enough. First-year students sometimes doubt that they will be able to meet the higher expectations of a final practicum. Realizing that this is happening will help you seek out support systems and listen to the positive comments made during evaluation conferences, so that you can go into interviews and exams from a position of strength. It is important to focus on the growth, joy, and positive experiences from the practicum as well as to deal with any losses and disappointments. For most people, the practicum experience is the most memorable part of their education. Recounting the positives—the satisfaction when a meeting went well; the sparkle in that client's eye; the strong relationship with your field instructor; the support and consultation from your faculty liaison and seminar members—adds a valuable perspective to the termination process.

PROCESS OF TERMINATION

The process of termination is like finishing a knitting project. A knitter needs to bind off and secure the yarn so the piece doesn't unravel and come undone—to prevent the planning, work, and effort from being lost. If it is the knitter's first piece, the finished project may have a few bumps and uneven corners, but the next project will likely show improvement. If it is an advanced project, the piece is likely more complex and has fewer obvious mistakes. As in knitting, ending the practicum involves attention both to small details and to the larger, completed work. The process of termination needs to begin early. This process includes building in the time to meet your emotional needs and to reflect on your growth and learning. We recommend a final conference with your field instructor and, when possible, the faculty liaison.   Table 9.1 is an outline of termination tasks for you to adapt to fit your needs.   Form 9.1 at the end of the chapter can be used for a written evaluation at the end of your placement.

Moving on: Life beyond Field

If you are planning another field placement, review the process for selecting a placement with your faculty liaison. Refer to Appendices A and B for suggestions and guidelines, checking to make certain they do not conflict with your program's policies. Ask how your field instructor is willing to be involved, for example, conducting a mock interview, reviewing your strengths, discussing areas of growth, or recommending potential practicum sites. As we mentioned earlier, our research has shown that students with a remaining practicum are often confident as they end the year. This may be because they are able to identify gaps and goals, and they plan to address them in their next practicum.

As you prepare to join the profession, plan how to become involved in the professional community. Consider membership in professional organizations such as NASW, National Association of Black Social Workers, a local group such as the Nursing Home Social Workers Association, Coalition of Licensed Social Workers, an AIDS task force, or a children's political action group.   Membership in professional organizations not only provides wonderful opportunities for learning about jobs and continuing educational opportunities, but also is a way to demonstrate your commitment to the profession and its goals.

TASKS FOR TERMINATION
Table 9.1

Beginning of Last Semester/Quarter

◊ Look over final evaluation forms
◊ Discuss learning contract and progress on goals
◊ Outline priorities and expectations for the time remaining

One to Two Months before Ending

◊ Set the ending date with field instructor
◊ Discuss remaining objectives and tasks to be completed
◊ Discuss the school's ending requirements (forms, conferences)
◊ Identify your feelings, needs, and issues in saying good-bye
◊ Identify your field instructor's feelings, needs, and issues in saying good-bye
◊ Discuss how you will plan to meet those needs
◊ Discuss the impact on you of leaving each client, group, community
◊ Discuss how to respond to emotional and behavioral reactions of clients and groups
◊ Discuss how to end with staff
◊ Discuss how to end your work - how to transfer cases, finish projects, write reports
◊ Identify others who need to know that you are leaving

Final Weeks before Ending

◊ Begin to say good-bye to clients, staff, and others
◊ Prepare for final evaluation conference
◊ Questions you might think about:
  1. What did you enjoy most? (this points to your skills)
  2. What area of growth are you most pleased about?
  3. What were the barriers/ challenges (what helped you overcome them?)
  4. How are you different now from when you began?
  5. What are your major strengths as a social worker?
  6. What comes next? (future growth and development needs)
◊ Plan also to give feedback to your field instructor about contributions to your learning and to make suggestions for changes if the agency/field instructor has another student.
◊ Discuss what ongoing contact you will have with your field instructor (will references be provided? are phone calls welcome?)
◊ Discuss what will be different if you are staying on as an employee/volunteer

Last Day

◊ Hand back the keys, identification tags, parking passes
◊ Complete any last-minute paperwork
◊ Say good-bye
◊ Celebrate your growth and learning

If your state licenses social workers, locate information about the exam, as well as supervision and continuing education requirements. Talk with faculty and students about how students have done in the various areas of the test, what to expect, and how to prepare. The process can be a lengthy one, so find out the requirements in advance of graduation. You may be eligible for some jobs only after you are licensed.

Job Search

If you are looking for a job, many resources are available to you. Most colleges and universities have career services which provide help writing a resume or cover letter, and perhaps even job listings. Check with your social work program to see what information and services may be available. There are also books on the market, job hotlines, and numerous electronic services to help with job search skills; NASW also has a service for members. Because so many resources are available, we will focus on two essential but neglected aspects of a job search - networking and support. Networking is the process of making connections with people, in this case people who will be helpful in your job search. Support is essential in this process, which is often longer than expected and sometimes frustrating. Social workers have the skills to network and build support; it is part of the process of empowerment. When we reflect on how essential and critical it is to the success of groups and individual clients, it becomes clear how critical it can be to our own efforts.

Networking began before you took your first social work class; families and friends can be valuable in building a professional network. Your professors and fellow students know the social work community and people you can contact. Attending conferences and seminars is a valuable way to meet people also. These people may not always be potential employers, but they can help you focus or broaden your search. People in field agencies are also good connections, as are members of clubs and organizations.

Informational interviews are an excellent way to build a network as well as to find out about agencies and the work they do.

The purpose of an informational interview is not to apply for a job but to learn more information from someone in a position of influence and authority. You may learn about training and qualifications, and about services to clients as well as hiring practices. They may even refer you to other key people. This process is time consuming and demanding, but may result in finding a job. One important reminder about networking, particularly informational interviews: Respect the people's time and willingness to talk with you. Thank-you notes and follow-up calls are as much a part of the process as face-to-face contact.

We have discussed the value of support throughout this book. When students leave school, they leave an extensive support system - all the students, classes, and seminars. Graduating students have found it helpful to form a group (perhaps an existing seminar or study group) and agree to meet together at regular intervals until the last member has secured a job. Many communities also have job search support groups. It is difficult to rely on family members or people we live with to provide all the support we need. Fellow social workers offer a degree of empathy and encouragement that others cannot. In addition, this group may be one of your best sources of information about job opportunities.

Continuing Your Education

If you are completing an associate degree, you may be planning to continue on for a bachelor's degree. You may want to interview working professionals and college representatives to select a quality program and learn about employment opportunities for various degrees. If you plan to continue in the field of social work, you will need information about state licensing requirements and whether programs are accredited by the Council on Social Work Accreditation.

Students finishing a bachelor's degree may want to consider graduate school if they have a strong academic record, the experience to integrate graduate course material, and a commitment to social work values and ethics. Personal maturity and self-awareness are prerequisites for graduate work. Some students may choose to attend graduate school because working may be a scarier alternative. Taking a risk and facing the harder challenge of professional employment helps students be more confident practitioners. Many schools, in fact, require at least two years of practice of all applicants. This gives students additional experience with a variety of agencies and issues so that they are not only more confident that social work is a good fit for them, but better learners when they invest in a graduate education.

If you plan to enter a graduate school immediately after earning a baccalaureate degree, plan to start gathering information before your senior year. Start the process early because it takes time to gather information, receive applications, write a personal statement, contact references, and take any admission tests that may be required. Many M.S.W. programs offer advanced standing to B.S.W. graduates from an accredited social work program. An excellent place to begin your research is by looking at the report published by the Council on Social Work Education, "Summary Information of Master of Social Work Programs" that lists all the graduate schools accredited by CSWE. You could begin to narrow your choices by focusing on the area of concentration you are interested in or a geographic area. Talking with practitioners who are graduates of different schools, as well as with faculty members, will give you additional valuable information.

Whatever your plans are, transitions are exciting, frightening, and powerful times. We encourage you to take the time to be reflective, ask questions, take risks, and move on with confidence. Social workers continue learning and growing throughout their professional lives. We encourage you to set new professional goals and evaluate those goals, as well as your progress, throughout your profession.

JOURNAL ASSIGNMENTS

9.1   Reflecting on Past Endings

Write about three different times when you left a relationship or job:

- What was easy each time?
- What was difficult each time?
- Are there any patterns you see? strengths? areas you avoid? handle poorly?

Write about what you have learned about yourself:

- What needs do you have as you plan for the endings at your practicum?
- How will you meet those needs?
- How will your patterns affect those you work with?

9.2   Updating Your Self-Assessment

Review the inventory of personal strengths and fit with social work from Journal Assignment 1.1. After your final evaluation, add to that list a new assessment of your strengths as a social worker and areas for continued growth.

9.3   Reviewing and Planning

- Review your learning style and what you discovered about yourself in your practicum setting.
- Review the patterns of highs and lows in your journal.
- Clarify what you have learned about what you want next in a practicum or job. Build on your strengths and take into consideration what you need to learn.

9.4   Updating Support System

Refer to the list of your support system from Journal Assignment 1.2. Add to it and plan to draw on these supports as you look for a job or make the transition to a new placement.

9.5 Networking

Start an organized system of keeping track of network possibilities. Use it to keep track of names, addresses, phone numbers, who gave you the referral and summary notes following conversations. Note potential people to contact for informational interviews.

SEMINAR ACTIVITIES

9.1 Ending Seminar Group

Plan closing activities for the seminar group. Discuss what the group members need for closure. Plan an ending evaluation and activities to celebrate your work together.

9.2 Role Playing Agency Endings

Each student identifies an aspect of closure they would like to work on - with clients, staff, or field instructor. Break into groups of three or four students. Choose the role you want to play. Have other members give feedback and suggestions. Try the role play again incorporating the suggestions.

9.3 Role Playing Job Interviews

Each student has a mock interview with another student acting as a prospective employer. Research commonly asked questions and difficult questions. Group members give comments and suggestions about responses.

9.4 Informational Interviewing

Invite several employers of social workers in your community to talk with your seminar group about job search skills and tips.

9.5 Writing a Resume

Share a draft of your resume with other seminar members and your faculty liaison. Incorporate their comments and ideas to strengthen your resume.

ADDITIONAL READINGS:

Bolles, R.N. (1997). *What color is your parachute? A Practical manual for job-hunters and career changers.* Berkeley, CA: Ten Speed Press.

Fortune, A.E. (1987). Grief only? Client and social workers reaction to termination. *Clinical Social Work Journal, 15*, 157-171.

Landers, S. (1994, October). Terminating: When it's over, is it? *NASW News,* 3-4.

Kubler-Ross, E. (1970). *On death and dying.* NY: Macmillan.

FIELD EVALUATION
Form 9.1

PROCESS:

• Individual reflection and a written narrative completed separately by both student and field instructor. The following format may be adapted for differences in field programs, agency placement, and student level. Use additional sheets as needed.

• A conference in which both the student's and field instructor's narratives are discussed together, and responses to them and written and signed. It is valuable for the faculty liaison to attend this final conference.

FORMAT:

I. General reflections. Provide a brief overview of the following:

• Successes to celebrate: What did the student enjoy most, what skills are strongest, what work is the student most proud of?

• Challenges: What barriers, disappointments, or challenges did the student encounter? How were they dealt with?

• What continuing professional goals are identified for the student as the student moves into another practicum or employment?

II.   For each learning goal, identify:

- Work completed and its quality
- Work not completed; reasons
- Learning outcomes for the student
- Areas identified for future learning

III.   Skill level

Central social work skills are listed in bold below, followed by specific
examples of that skill. In a narrative, summarize the student's abilities for
each skill, giving concrete examples of behaviors to illustrate.

A. Self awareness and professional use of self
*Identifying own values and feelings, personal issues, strengths, limitations
*becoming aware of how these personal traits are perceived by and impact
others; *using these qualities intentionally and purposefully in work with
others; *engaging in increasing self-awareness; *understanding own style
and developing flexible repertoire

B. Communication skills
*Listening carefully to obtain reliable information; *demonstrating professional use of information and confidentiality; *demonstrating understanding and use of nonverbal communication; *showing empathy; *being able to discuss difficult issues; *communicating orally in clear, respectful, and congruent manner; *communicating in writing in a clear, concise, accurate, and organized manner; *being able to articulate and assert needs and opinions appropriately; *demonstrating skills in negotiation

C. Social work values and ethics
*Identifying values and ethics key to the profession; *recognizing and analyzing ethical dilemmas; *identifying own motives; *demonstrating skills in analyzing ethical issues; * identifying with and applying social work values and ethics in practice

D. Diversity
*Identifying and appreciating differences as strengths, *being aware of own diversity and one's impact on others; *being aware of effects of oppression on diverse populations; *working to enhance one's cultural awareness, knowledge, and competence; *identifying impact of diversity in individual's, families', groups, communities, tasks

E. Social work role and practice
*Articulating and implementing role of social worker in agency setting;
*articulating agency mission, program goals, purpose of social work tasks;
*demonstrating skills in working purposefully with others: engaging
clients/consumers/constituents, assessing strengths, needs, and issues, setting
appropriate goals in collaboration and working toward those goals, making
revisions and evaluating outcomes; ending working relationships and
identifying impact of endings; *developing knowledge of resources and ease
in referral; *understanding the impact and interplay of multiple systems;
*applying social work ethics and values in work on all levels

F. Work skills
*Effectively organizing time, work, tools, resources; *arriving reliably on
time and prepared; *demonstrating accountability for work assigned;
*understanding the roles of others in agency systems; *understanding agency
policy, procedures, culture; *critically evaluating agency practices; *using
agency processes for decision making and review; *identifying impact of
change and stress in agency; *collaborating, team building; *effectively
setting, monitoring, revising, and evaluating work goals; *making use of
support and consultation networks;   *being aware of own stress and effective
management of stress; *showing initiative; *being able to handle unexpected;
*being able to provide clear, constructive feedback

G. Skills in supervision and learning
*Understanding purpose of professional supervision; *attending conferences regularly, on time, and prepared; *Utilizing supervision to explore strengths and areas for future growth; *taking appropriate risks to extend one's skills; *identifying needed information and skills and resources available to increase knowledge; *demonstrating skills in handling success, failure, vulnerability, evaluation; *making use of others' wisdom and skills as learning resources; *seeking feedback, evaluating and responding to feedback; *applying material from coursework; *being willing to confront difficult issues; *having appropriate expectations of self; *accepting direction; *balancing tasks and process; *being aware of issues of authority and autonomy; *making appropriate use of support; *being able to sum up learning and growth to formulate plan for continued learning

IV. Summarize feedback to others:

- To field program and field liaison: What aspects of the program worked well? What did not work well? What changes are suggested for future placements?

- To agency: How is the agency effectively supporting field education? What barriers or difficulties exist? What changes are suggested for future placements at this agency?

- To field instructor: What aspects of orientation, assignments, and supervision work well? What did not work well? What changes are suggested for future placements with this field instructor?

V. Responses to evaluation

Field instructor response to student's evaluation:

_____   _____
Field Instructor signature   Date

Student's response to field instructor's evaluation:

_____   _____
Student signature   Date

Appendices

Appendices A-E provide guidance in the process of finding, interviewing, and selecting field placements. They are designed for students whose programs do not have these procedures or processes in place. While other students may also find this information useful, they should check to be sure these suggestions do not conflict with existing program policies.

Appendix A: Steps to Finding a Field Placement

1. **Learn what your program requires of agencies and field instructors.**
   A social work degree? License? Years of experience? To sign a contract? Attend orientation or training? Refer also to the expectations of agencies and field instructors in Chapter One. You want to ascertain whether an agency is interested in providing structure and support as you develop.

2. **Use a variety of ways to locate potential agencies.**
   Use Yellow Pages, community social service directories, faculty, friends, contacts from workshops or meetings, and suggestions made by agencies themselves in the process of interviewing. Get names of specific social workers. Learn something about the agency before the interview so you can ask questions.

3. **Prepare an application.**
   Use the form provided by your program or the sample in Appendix C. An attractive application provides concrete information about you; highlights your strengths, interests, and goals; and demonstrates professionalism.

4. **Practice courtesy in contacting agencies.**
   Identify yourself and give the name of your college and your level, and explain that you are exploring practicum possibilities. Explain that you are looking for a practicum placement that meets your school's requirements. Ask what kind of experience they might be able to provide to a social work student.

5. **Be prepared to answer the agency's immediate questions.**
   Agencies unfamiliar with your program could be expected to ask:

   • What are you interested in doing?
   • How many months would you be committing to the agency?
   • How many hours a week would you work?
   • Do we have to pay you?
   • If I'm not a social worker, can I be your field instructor?
   • What will this entail from me?

6. **Ask for an interview and prepare carefully for it.**
   See suggestions in Appendix B. Bring copies of any material provided by your program that would be useful to the field instructor.

7. **Clarify what questions the agency has.**
   Find answers for them or connect them with faculty who can help. Explain what remains of your placement process and indicate when you will contact them again.

8. **Be familiar with the approval or placement selection process at your social work program.**
   Follow the placement procedures carefully and call faculty to clarify any questions.

Copyright © 1999 by Allyn and Bacon.

Appendix B: Interviewing with an Agency

1. Prepare answers to questions the agency might ask.

Questions You May Be Asked in a Field Interview

Why are you interested in this agency/program?

What strengths do you bring to this specific work?

Why do you want to be a social worker?

What would you hope to learn here?

What are you looking for in a field instructor?

How do you like to use supervisory conferences?

Tell me more about your previous experience.

What experiences with diverse populations have you had?

What social work class is your favorite?

What social work class has been especially challenging for you?

Describe your learning - or work - style.

How well do you work on a team?

How do you handle stress?

Do you have any personal experience with the issues we work with here
(domestic violence, child abuse, alcoholism, adoption, grief & loss)?

Tell me about a specific case or project you have worked with.

How many hours and what specific days could you commit to being here? For
how long?

---

2. Plan the questions that you want to ask. This is your opportunity to learn about this agency and its services and to assess how well it fits with your needs and interests. Here are some questions to get you started. Adapt them and add questions to fit your needs.

Questions You May Want to Ask in a Field Interview

What is your experience with this school/other students?

Why are you considering having a student?

What do you expect from a student?

How would you describe your supervisory style?

What would a supervision session with you be like?

Are you available for informal supervision other than the time scheduled?

What would a typical day be like?

How did you get into this field, and what do you enjoy about it?

What kind of orientation is planned for a student?

Are there other staff I would be working closely with? If so, will I be able to

    meet them?

Can I talk with other students that you've had?

What hours do you expect a student to have?

Are there meetings which I am required to attend?

How do you address the issue of safety in this agency?

Will I need a car? If so who pays for mileage and insurance?

---

3. **Dress appropriately.** Dress as you would if you were interviewing for the social work position at that agency.

4. **Arrive on time.** Get directions to the agency and find out where to park. You may want to drive by in advance. Arrive a few minutes early so that you can be ready when the field instructor is available. Spend those minutes breathing deeply if you are anxious, reviewing your application and list of strengths, or observing the agency. If you are late, apologize and explain what held you up.

5. **Be respectful of the field instructor's time.** Find out how much time is available to meet with you. Keep an eye on the clock and stop on time. If you don't finish, ask when it would be convenient to call.

6. **Expect the unexpected.** There will probably be a question that surprises you. It is just fine to say, "Let me think about that" or "I don't know how to answer." Sometimes people want to see how you handle a stressful situation. Others may want to know what personal issues may get in the way of working with their clients. Since this is not a job interview, there are not the same guidelines regarding "illegal" questions, for example, about your marital status, sexual orientation, religion, or disabilities. If you feel the question was inappropriate, you may ask how that fits with this experience. If you have personal issues that may affect your work with clients, talk with your faculty liaison about how to prepare for an interview. You are not required to discuss personal issues, but you do need to be honest with yourself and your potential field instructor.

7. **After the interview - reflect.** What questions did you answer well, what questions do you wish you had asked, and what question were you unprepared for or wish you had answered differently? Think about how you felt at the agency, with the field instructor, and about the possibility of learning there. Jot down your thoughts and questions to help prepare you for other interviews and to help you decide among agencies.

8. **Follow up.** It is always appropriate to send a thank you note. Even though you may not be assigned to that agency, it is very possible that in the future you may be working with them or even applying for a job there.

9. **Get help in dealing with disappointments.** An agency you really want may not select you. Finding out more about their reasons may help you resolve feelings of rejection. Perhaps they had twenty students apply and only had room for one; perhaps they picked up on personal, unresolved issues that would get in the way of the work; perhaps you could have presented yourself differently and they are willing to give you feedback that would make you a stronger candidate for another placement. Ask your faculty liaison how to get this information.

10. **Making a decision.** So many issues must be considered in making a final decision about a placement; it is not unusual for students to find themselves consumed - even obsessed - for days at a time. The Decision Map in Appendix E may help you to map out the flood of factors confronting you as you move toward your practicum choice.

Appendix C - APPLICATION FOR SOCIAL WORK FIELD POSITION

_____
(Name)

_____
(Address)

_____
(Phone Number)

EDUCATION

_____
(Present College)

_____
(City, State)

_____
(Expected date of graduation)

_____
(Previous College)

_____
(City, State)

_____
(Dates of Attendance)

EXPERIENCE
(Employment and Voluntary Service)

_____
(Agency/Organization -- present or most recent)

_____
(Job Title)   (Dates of Employment)
Responsibilities:_____
_____
_____

_____

(Agency/Organization)

_____

(Job Title)   (Dates of Employment)

Responsibilities:_____

_____

_____

_____

PERSONAL INFORMATION

My strengths as a social worker:

My limitations as a social worker:

My general goals for fieldwork:

Additional information of importance for an interviewer to know about me:

Names and phone numbers of references or contacts (Field Administrator, Faculty, Advisor, etc.):

Appendix D: Field Practicum in Place of Employment

Professional employment and learning are not inconsistent, but there is a difference of emphasis between the roles of students and staff and the balance between the goals of educational development and delivery of service to clients. CSWE Standards emphasize new learning and do not allow giving credit for previous work. The standards for the practicum in place of employment must be the same as for a practicum in any other agency: The qualifications of the field instructor must be met and assignments must be consistent with the educational objectives of the program and must reflect an educational design and the student's learning needs.

A signed agreement is a valuable tool to confirm that there is knowledge of and agreement to the employee taking on a learner role, to agree on new learning assignments, and to reflect qualifications of field instructor.

ISSUES TO CONSIDER WHEN THINKING OF PRACTICUM IN PLACE OF EMPLOYMENT

Start the process of discussion early. A good practicum takes time to create.

1. The changing relationship: The authority of the new field instructor will be different and must be discussed. If the student and proposed field instructor are/have been colleagues, how will the transition to a different relationship be handled?

2. The relationship with coworkers: If the workload for coworkers will change when the student takes on the student status, this must be addressed. How will the student's coworkers respond? How will they be prepared for the change in the student's responsibilities? How will this be communicated? Are they prepared to share clients? Can the student/employee observe them?

3. Student role versus employee role: The challenge for many "student" employees is to divide the work between "student learning" and "employee duties." It is important to reflect in the education contract what work will be part of the learning objectives and why. The education contract will help to clarify which hours may be counted toward field hours. Does the agency support clearly

defining the hours as "work" and "student" hours? If not, how will the student hours be tracked?

If the student is to be physically sitting at the same desk when completing the student role as when in the employee role, the potential for interruptions and blurring of roles is greater than if the student is at a completely different work site. How will fellow workers and clients know when the "employee" is wearing the "student" hat and not ask about "employee" issues?

4. Permission to be a student: One of the luxuries of being a student is the freedom to make mistakes and to be encouraged to take risks and learn. If the student is seen as a competent worker, this risk taking is often hampered. How will the permission be given to make mistakes? How will the image of the employee/student be affected? How would concerns about practice be handled - involve the faculty liaison? discuss with the employer?

FIELD PRACTICUM AGREEMENT IN PLACE OF EMPLOYMENT

1. Agency Name _____
   Agency Address _____

2. Executive Director/Administrator Name _____

3. Student Name _____
   Length of Employment _____

4. Student's present employment status and job description:
   _____
   _____
   _____

5. Type of assignments/work responsibilities student presently has:
   _____
   _____
   _____
   _____

6. Type of new assignments student will be given as part of work study arrangement:
   _____
   _____
   _____
   _____

7. What will be the new or changing emphasis in the student's work study placement?
   _____
   _____
   _____
   _____

8. Student's work study time will consist of _____ days per week, totaling _____ hours, in addition to any other time student may be in agency as part of ongoing employment.

9. Student's present supervisor (or equivalent)

    _____

10. Proposed Field Instructor

    _____

This Agreement meets the approval of the Agency Director, Field Instructor, the Student and Faculty Liaison or School's Director of Field.

Agency Executive Director _____

Agency Supervisor _____

Agency Field Instructor _____

Student _____

Faculty Liaison _____

Director of Field Education _____

Source: Adapted with permission from University of Denver Graduate School of Social Work.

Appendix E: Decision Map

The factors that go into choosing a field placement can be arranged along poles of personal-professional and internal-external. Personal factors are those mostly unique to you and may involve internal factors related to your personality, or external factors related to your environmental situation and concrete resources. Professional factors are those dealing directly with your development in the field of social work. Again, they may be mostly internal, such as your own goals and preferences, or they may be external requirements or limitations.

As you map the factors in your own specific case, you will find that each quadrant speaks with different voices. On the personal half of the map you may hear your own voice speaking about your dreams, your hopes, and even fears and anxieties you experience in other contexts. It is critical to listen to this subjective side in order to refine your self-awareness and professional plans. On the external side the voices press in from all around. You may hear your parent's concerns for your safety, your children questioning if you'll be late again tonight, even your car mechanic's dire predictions! You will also be able to pay attention, hopefully, to those people concerned that you get the best possible experience to foster your professional development. Let their years of field experience enter the mix and advocate for your learning.

The best choices consider all quadrants of the map. Each student will be unique, however, in how heavily some quadrants weigh in the decision making. A brand new baby may certainly dominate your attention. A small rural area will probably present limited agency choices. However, when one quadrant begins to dominate it may be time to step back to listen for other voices. Perhaps you have a driving ambition to work with handicapped children and only handicapped children. Balance this with your program's expectations that you develop generalist skills. If your decision is being dominated by your fear of the inner city, spend some time reflecting on what may lay behind that fear, and tallying up the strengths and resources that could support you if you took the risk to try a new experience.

Decision Map: Factors Involved in Choosing a Field Placement

Professional

Professional goals and interests
"Clicking" with field instructor
Preferences for
   types of work
   clients
   fields of practice
Perceptions or reactions to
   agency
   neighborhood
Past experience

Availability of
   agencies
   field instructors
Social work program
   goals
   structure
   processes
   timelines
   requirements

Internal

Personal issues
Learning style
Strengths
Limitations
Fears/needs

Environmental resources
Transportation issues
Time, schedule
Availability
Your support network
Expectations of others
Family demands

External

Personal

179

NASW Code of Ethics
Adopted August, 1996 - Effective January, 1997

Overview

The NASW *Code of Ethics* is intended to serve as a guide to the everyday professional conduct of social workers. This *Code* includes four sections. The first Section, "Preamble," summarizes the social work profession's mission and core values. The second section, "Purpose of the *NASW Code of Ethics*," provides an overview of the *Code's* main functions and a brief guide for dealing with ethical issues or dilemmas in social work practice. The third section, "Ethical Principles," presents broad ethical principles, based on social work's core values, that inform social work practice. The final section, "Ethical Standards," includes specific ethical standards to guide social workers' conduct and to provide a basis for adjudication.

Preamble

The primary mission of the social work profession is to enhance human well-being and help meet the basic human needs of all people, with particular attention to the needs and empowerment of people who are vulnerable, oppressed, and living in poverty. A historic and defining feature of social work is the profession's focus on individual well-being in a social context and the well-being of society. Fundamental to social work is attention to the environmental forces that create, contribute to, and address problems in living.

Social workers promote social justice and social change with and on behalf of clients. "Clients" is used inclusively to refer to individuals, families, groups, organizations, and communities. Social workers are sensitive to cultural and ethnic diversity and strive to end discrimination, oppression, poverty, and other forms of social injustice. These activities may be in the form of direct practice, community organizing, supervision, consultation, administration, advocacy, social and political action, policy development and implementation, education, and research and evaluation. Social workers seek to enhance the capacity of people to address their own needs. Social workers also seek to promote the responsiveness of organizations, communities, and other social institutions to individuals' needs and social problems.

The mission of the social work profession is rooted in a set of core values. These core values, embraced by social workers throughout the profession's history, are the foundation of social work's unique purpose and perspective:
- service
- social justice
- dignity and worth of the person
- importance of human relationships
- integrity
- competence

This constellation of core values reflects what is unique to the social work profession. Core values, and the principles that flow from them, must be balanced within the context and complexity of the human experience.

NASW Ethical Principles

The following ethical principles are based on social work's core values of service, social justice, dignity and worth of the person, importance of human relationships, integrity, and competence. These principles set forth ideals to which all social workers should aspire.

Value: *Service*
Ethical Principle: *Social workers' primary goal is to help people in need and to address social problems.*

Social workers elevate service to others above self-interest. Social workers draw on their knowledge, values, and skills to help people in need and to address social problems. Social workers are encouraged to volunteer some portion of their professional skills with no expectation of significant financial return (pro bono service).

Value: *Social Justice*
Ethical Principle: *Social workers challenge social injustice.*

Social workers pursue social change, particularly with and on behalf of vulnerable and oppressed individuals and groups of people. Social workers' social change efforts are focused primarily on issues of poverty, unemployment, discrimination, and other forms of social injustice. These activities seek to promote sensitivity to and knowledge about oppression and cultural and ethnic diversity. Social workers strive to ensure access to needed information, services, and resources; equality of opportunity; and meaningful participation in decision-making for all people.

Value: *Dignity and Worth of the Person*
Ethical Principle: *Social workers respect the inherent dignity and worth of the person.*

Social workers treat each person in a caring and respectful fashion, mindful of individual differences and cultural and ethnic diversity. Social workers promote clients' socially responsible self-determination. Social workers seek to enhance clients' capacity and opportunity to change and address their own needs. Social workers are cognizant of their dual responsibility to clients and to the broader society. They seek to resolve conflicts between clients' interests and the broader society's interests in a socially responsible manner consistent with the values, ethical principles, and ethical standards of the profession.

Value: *Importance of Human Relationships*
Ethical Principle: *Social workers recognize the central importance of human relationships.*

Social workers understand that relationships between and among people are an important vehicle for change. Social workers engage people as partners in the helping process. Social workers seek to strengthen relationships among people in a purposeful effort to promote, restore, maintain, and enhance the well-being of individuals, families, social groups, organizations, and communities.

Value: *Integrity*
Ethical Principle: *Social workers behave in a trustworthy manner.*

Social workers are continually aware of the profession's mission, values, ethical principles, and ethical standards and practice in a manner consistent with them. Social workers act honestly and responsibly and promote ethical practices on the part of the organizations with which they are affiliated.

Value: *Competence*
Ethical Principle: *Social workers practice within their areas of competence and develop and enhance their professional experience.*

Social workers continually strive to increase their professional knowledge and skills and to apply them in practice. Social workers should aspire to contribute to the knowledge base of the profession.

Sources for additional Codes of Ethics:

National Association of Black Social Workers:
c/o Columbia University School of Social Work, 622 West 113 Street, New York, NY 10025.

North American Association of Christians in Social Work (NACSW):
PO Box 1212, Botsford, CT 06404-0121

International Code of Ethics for the Professional Social Worker:
Van Soest, D. (1992). *Incorporating peace and social justice into the social work curriculum* (pp. 187-188). Washington, DC: National Association of Social Workers, Peace and Social Justice Committee.

American Association for Marriage and Family Therapy:
1133 Fifteenth Street, NW, Suite 300, Washington, DC 20005.

American Association for Counseling and Development:
5999 Stevenson Avenue, Alexandria, VA, 22304

Canadian Association of Social Workers:
383 Parkdale Avenue, Suite 402, Ottowa, K1Y4R4, Canada.

Index

A

accountability and documentation, 140
accountability, agency, 31
accreditation, of social work programs, 6
administration, see agency, administration
adult learner, vignettes, 4, 21, 71, 76
advocacy, 142
age differences in supervision, 75-76, vignette, 71
agency
administration, 137, 139, 144
changing placement in, 97
choosing an, 168-171
cultural competence in, 135-7
diversity in, 44
expectations, 9
information and orientation, 27
mission, 30, 61
orientation and staff, 28-29
orientation to services, 29
policy and supervision, 138-9
policy, 9, 143
presentation outline, 37
presentation, 33
social work role in, 25, 60-61
structure, 28
see also deciding on field placement
Alberti, R.E., 82
Alvarez A.R., 145
anxiety, ii, 58
application for field position, 172-173
assertiveness, 12, 44, 91-92, 141
assessing
agency possibilities, 43
personal needs, 44
program requirements, 43
attitudes and diversity, 135
authority and power
experiences with, 81
in learning contract, 45
authority and supervision, 75
Ayers, J., 78

B

Barretta-Herman, A., 82
Bates, M., 19
Becerra R.M., 39
Beginning Agreement, 25, 35

Beginning stage, vi, 2, 20, 40, 56
beginning work, 58
beginnings, importance of, 23
Berger, B. 127, 129
Berger, S.S., 39
Bobo, K.,145
Bogo, M., 39
Bolles, R.N., 159
Borrup, J., 19, 23, 39
boundaries, 13-14, 87, 112
vignettes, 3, 109-110
with clients, 112
with field instructors, 87, 112
Brill, N.L., 69
Bucholz, E.S., 39

C

Callanan, P., 129
case presentation, see consultation, peer request form
challenges, 99, 134, see also difficult issues
changing field instructors, 96
changing placements, 97
choosing an agency, 168-171, 178-179
Chuck, F., 39
classism, 133
clients
learning from, 17
first, 58
preparing for, 58, 63
closure
developmental stage, vii, 146
importance of, 99, 149-150
see also termination
Cochrane, S., 5, 127, 129
code of ethics, 118, 120-123, 123, 182-184
collaboration, 140
communities
orientation to, 30
types of, 30
competence, 108, 111
confidence, 132, 134
confidentiality, 29, 99, 120
conflict, 97, see also confrontation
confrontation, 87, 91
consultation
importance of, 89
peer request form, 105
peer, 102, 125
purposes of, 90-91
sources of, 89-90

versus supervision, 89
Corey G., 129
Corey M., 129
Council on Social Work Education, 6, 7,
    10
counter transference, 112
Covey, S.R., 145
Cross, T.L., 134, 145
Cultural Competence Continuum, 136
cultural competence
    and agencies, 135-137, 143-144
    and learning contract, 46
    and self awareness, 135-137, 143
    in supervision, 59-60
cultural differences, 44, 59-60
    difficult issues and, 87
    in vignettes, 3, 41, 57, 110

D
Davis, M., 107
deciding on a field placement, 168-171
decision making, factors in agency, 138
decision map, 178-179
developmental process
    Beginning, 2, 20, 40, 56
    chart, vi, vii
    Closure, 146
    differences & similarities, i, ii, 5
    graduate students, ii
    in field i, iii, iv
    juniors, ii
    Reality Confrontation, 70, 84
    Relative Mastery, 108, 132
    seniors, ii
Dietz, T.J., 130
differences
    and social work practice, 134
    appreciating, 11
    workplace, 134
difficult issues
    effects on learning and practice,
        60, 87
    examples, 88
DiTiberio, J.K., 19
diversity
    age, 21, 71, 75-76
    class, 109, 133
    cultural, *see* cultural differences
    gender, 41
    resources to learn about, 52
    sexual orientation, 3, 85
    spirituality and, 110, 115
    worker attitudes, 135

documentation, 140
    and orientation, 27
Dolgoff, R., 129
dress, 171
dual relationships, 112-113

E
eco-maps, 15
Emmons, M.L., 82
empathy, *see* tuning in
employee, versus student role, 6-7
employment, practicum in place of, 174-
    177
endings, handling, 149,
        see also closure *or* termination
Erlish, J.L., 39
Eshelman, E.R., 107
ethical analysis, 91, 141-142
ethical decision making
    model, 119
    process, 120-123, 125
ethical dilemmas, 118
evaluation
    form, 159
    in learning contract, 48-49
    midpoint, 82
    of individual participation in
seminar, 100-101
    of practice, 123, 125
    of seminar group, 102-3
    ongoing, 63-65
    vulnerability in, 63-64
expectations
    of self, 10
    reasonable, 92

F
faculty liaison
    definition, 8
    expectations of, 8-9
feedback
    active practice and, 116
    in the beginning, 14, 63-64
    reactions to, 78
    relative mastery and, 116
    skills in 78
    SPIN guidelines for, 79
    tools, 64
field agencies, criteria for selecting, 7
field instruction in place of employment,
see employment
field instruction, *see* supervision
field instructor

changing, 96
 definition, 8
 expectations of, 9
 functions, 9
field programs
 requirements, 43
 differences in, 7
field seminars, *see* seminars
first day experiences, 3-4, 21-22, 31, 32
Fisher, R., 107
Five Ws in orientation, 24
Fortune, A.E., 159
Frankl, V.E., 129
Freed, A.O., 69

G

Gambrill, E., 129
Ginsberg, L.H., 19
Glassman U., 82
goals and objectives of field program, 9
gossip, 97
graduate education, 155-6
Graybill, C.T., 53
grievance procedure, 99
Grossman B., 82
group
 development, seminar, 86
 norms, seminar 8-9, 18
Gutierrez, L., 145

H

Hamel R., 119, 129
Hammer, A.L., 19
harassment, *see* sexual harassment
Harrison D.F., 53
Hepworth D.H., 129
Herman, W.R., 19, 23
Human behavior in the social
 environment, integrated with
 field, 59

I

I messages and supervision, 78
illness, 71
independence and supervision, 74-75
informational interviews, 154-155, 158
Inglehart A.P., 39
insurance, 170
integration and learning, 5
internet, 144-145
internship, see field
interviewing

field agency, 169-171
 learning contract and, 45
 preparing for, *see* client, first

J

Jacobs, C., 107
job search, resources for, 154
Johnson, D.W., 19, 82, 107
Johnston, N., 82
journal, suggestions for keeping, 4
 see also journal assignments,
 end of each chapter

K

Kaiser, T.L., 82
Kazmerski, K.J., 5
Keirsey, D., 19
Kendal, J., 145
Kubler-Ross, E., 159
Kuechler, C.F., 107
Kutchins, H., 53

L

Landers, S., 159
learner role, 12
learner, adult, vignettes, 4, 21
learning contract
 planning, 47
 balance in, 49-51
 form, 53
 purposes of, 44
 sample of, 45-6
learning styles, i, 12, 16, 19, 32
 orientation and, 25
leaving social work, 98
leaving the agency, *see* changing
 placements *or* termination
legal issues and orientation, 27
legislation, 31
 in learning contract, 46
Leigh, J.W., 145
Lerner, H.G., 107
Lewis, E., 145
licensing, 154
losses and closure, 149
Lowenberg, F., 129
Lum D., 53

M

macro level
 active practice on, 116-117
 orientation on, 27, 29-31

Madrigal C., 145
Master of Social Work (MSW) programs, 156
mastery, *see* Relative Mastery
Max, S., 145
May L., 129
Maypole, D.E., 107
McKay, M., 107
McLaughlin, F.X., 107
McMurtry, S.L., 39
mezzo level
    active practice on, 116-7
    orientation on, 26, 28-9
micro level
    active practice on, 116-7
    orientation on, 24-28
Millan A., 145
mistakes, learning from, 14, vignette, 85
model, ethical decision making, 119

N

NASW 118, 154
NASW Code of Ethics, 182-183
negotiation
    difficult issues and, 92-93
    feedback and, 79
    in supervision, 59
    process, 92
    skills, 141
Nemon H., 145
Netting F.E., 39
networking, 154-155, 158

O

observation, 25
    in learning contract, 45
organizational change, 142
organizational structure, 28, 137
orientation
    learning styles and, 25
    macro level, 27, 29-31
    mezzo level, 26, 28-29
    micro level, 24-28
    plan, 26
    value of, 23

P

paperwork, 9, 29, 140
Perlman H.H., 69
personal development, sources of 111
personal issues
    effect on practice 111-112, 124

ethical model and, 122
    in vignette, 109
    self awareness, 15
personal needs, in learning contract, 51
personal style, 114, 124
    clues to understanding, 113, 124
policy
    agency, 137-138
    course, integration with field, 144
    learning contract, 46
Pollack, D., 107
power
    authority and, 81
    experiences with, 81
    supervision and, 76
practice
    active, 115
    analytical, 118
    aware, 111
    course, integration with field, 63, 66
    interviewing skills, 63
practicum instructor
    see field instructor
practicum, *see* field
preparing to learn, 4
process recordings, 64
professional
    behavior, 124, 127
    development, 111
    involvement, 151
    use of self, 13, 117
Prueger, R., 129

R

Reality Confrontation, vi, 70, 84
Reamer F., 107, 129
recontracting, 93
recording, *see* documentation
    or process recordings
Reitmeir, M.A., 82
relationships
    dual, 111-112
    supervisory
        see supervision relationships
    with clients, 112
    with staff, 143
Relative Mastery, vii, 108, 132
research
    applying in field, 125
    course, integration with field, 49, 123

in practice, 123-4
on field development, i
resources
for learning contract, 46, 52
orientation, 27
respect, 140
resume, 159
reviewing work, 63, see also evaluation
Rhodes, M.L., 130
Richard, R., 107
risks, 133
Rivard, J.D., 145
Rodway, M.R., 107
role, explaining social work, 62, 65
roleplay
difficult situations, 102
endings, 158
feedback, 81
job interview, 158
Rooney, R., 82
Ruff, E., 153

S

safety, 29, 88
Saleebey, D., 19
Schneck D., 82
Schwartz G., 53
self-awareness
closure and, 149, 157
cultural competence and, 134-137, 143
learning contract and, 44
personal issues and, 13, 117, 124,
vignette 109-110
self-disclosure, vignette, 3-4, 13-14
Semabeikian, P., 130
seminar groups, field, 8, 32, 81, 100
ending, 158
reality confrontation in, 86
sexual harassment
examples, 95
steps to handle, 96
sexual involvement with clients, 112
Shank, B., 95
Sharratt, S.H., 129
Shulman, L., 61, 69
sickness, 71
skills for confronting difficult issues, 91
skills, workplace, 139
social work
fit with, 17, 98
functions, 61

leaving, 98
role and agency decision making 138
role, 41, 61, 65, 66
values, 65, see also values
spirituality and professional growth 115, 124,
see also diversity
strengths
building on student, 10, 14, 51, 157
client, 59
community, 27
stress management, 93-94, 100
style, personal, 114
Sue D., 145
Sue D.W., 145
supervision
agency policy and, 138-9
authority and, 75
components of, 73
cultural differences and, 59-60
I messages in, 78
improving, 76
in Beginning stage, 63-4
in orientation, 24, 32
independence and, 74-5
negotiation and, 59
power and, 76
preparing for sessions, 77
see also boundaries
support and, 13, 73-74
taking risks and, 142
task and process in, 76
tuning in during, 60
understanding, 72
versus friendship, 74
supervisor, responsibilities of, 72-73
support
after field placement, 155
in supervision, 73-4
systems, 15, 81, 157

T

taping, audio, 64
team-building, 140
technology, see internet
termination
process of, 150
tasks, 152-3
Thornton, S., 5, 127, 129
Thyer, B.S., 53
tolerance, 140

transference,   112
tuning in, 59, 61

U
Uehara, E.S., 130
unspoken messages, 62
Ury, W., 107

V
value differences, tuning in to, 60, 63
values, social work, 9
Verson, G.,39
volunteer, versus student role, 6-7, 153
vulnerable, feeling, 2, 21, 64

W
Weil, M.O., 145
Westerfeldt, A., 130
whistle blowing, 142-143
Wilson, S.J., 53
Wodarski, J.S., 53
work presentation, 67-8
workplace
       differences, in, 134
       dynamics, 137
       skills, 139